Richard Hoare
& Andrew Gummer

Do Deal

Negotiate better.
Find hidden value.
Enrich relationships.

BooK Co

Published by
The Do Book Company 2022
Works in Progress Publishing Ltd
thedobook.co

Text © Richard Hoare,
Andrew Gummer 2022
Illustrations © Hannah Cousins 2022

The right of Richard Hoare and Andrew
Gummer to be identified as authors of
this work has been asserted by them
in accordance with the Copyright,
Designs and Patents Act 1988

All rights reserved. No part of this
publication may be reproduced,
stored in or introduced to a retrieval
system, or transmitted in any form or
by any means (electronic, mechanical,
photocopying, recording or otherwise)
without the prior written permission of
the publisher. Requests for permission
should be sent to: info@thedobook.co

To find out more about our company,
books and authors, please visit
thedobook.co or follow us **@dobookco**

5 per cent of our proceeds from the sale
of this book is given to The Do Lectures
to help it achieve its aim of making
positive change: **thedolectures.com**

Cover designed by James Victore
Book designed and set by Ratiotype

Printed and bound by OZGraf Print
on Munken, an FSC-certified paper

A CIP catalogue record for this book
is available from the British Library

ISBN 978-1-914168-04-8

10 9 8 7 6 5 4 3 2 1

Contents

Prologue

Richard has been working as a music lawyer for about 20 years, Andrew has been doing the same job for even longer. Every day, we negotiate all sorts of deals with all sorts of wild and wonderful people, representing highly successful artists, record labels and businesses in, sometimes, extremely high-stakes negotiations. But Richard's first experience of negotiation in the music industry wasn't a particularly impressive one.

Putney Bridge, January 2000

It was the Millennium and the world hadn't ended due to a glitch in the matrix but, rather depressingly, Irish boyband Westlife were still at number one (just as they had been in December 1999) with a grimly forgettable cover version of Abba's 'I Have a Dream'.

Richard was doing a law degree at the time and was looking for a work placement for the third 'sandwich' year of the course. He had an interview lined up with the director of legal and business affairs at a major record label (the same label as Westlife were signed to, in fact) — a very experienced and formidable lawyer called Clive Rich.

Richard was 21 at the time, fresh from the rolling hills of Dartmoor where he grew up, via a sleepy seaside university town. This interview represented his first-ever real-life negotiation in the cut-and-thrust music industry.

So, how did he do?

Pretty badly as it turns out.

He did get the job, but when the question of salary came up, Clive proposed that he would be paid — wait for it — £6,000 for the year. Even in the year 2000, that was a pittance to live on in central London.

How did he respond to this incredibly low opening offer?

He simply accepted it. No questions asked. No negotiation at all really. (To be fair, Clive did go on to write a bestselling guide to negotiation, *The Yes Book*).

So, Richard had a foot in the door, barely — but as far as first negotiation experiences are concerned, it was a disaster. On the train back to university that day, he felt it was a missed opportunity to prove his negotiation chops, by haggling the salary up a little bit at least.

He had 'lost' this negotiation.

Fast-forward 20 years

A lot has happened. Richard made it through his year's work placement at the record label. One of the lawyers in the department introduced him to some people at the specialist music law firm where he had trained, called Clintons, the oldest and best music law firm in London. Richard managed to get a training contract there after completing law school and spent the next 12 years working at Clintons, alongside some of the most skilful and accomplished lawyers and negotiators in the music business.

He got to travel the world and was part of a team who advised many of his musical heroes from the world of electronic and dance music, as they represented the likes of Daft Punk, Aphex Twin and Jamiroquai.

After his sons were born, he decided to move back to the West Country to be closer to family, and in 2015 started his own practice in Frome, Somerset, with a small roster of artists.

By 2020, Richard's firm has become more established, and some of the clients are doing quite well. So, he finds himself at the boardroom table of another major record label, for another negotiation, only this time the stakes are much higher.

One of the artists they work with has spent most of the summer at number one in the charts with a huge hit single (to up the ante even more, it was also his youngest son's favourite song).

The client's proposed record contract is in front of him and there are some crucial issues that need to be negotiated. If they don't resolve them here and now, the artist's career could be over before it starts — it's now or never. Sat opposite are the heads of the label, plus their team of ferocious lawyers.

How would he fare in this negotiation compared to the one 20 years ago?

Well, this time things go far better. Because in the time that has passed, he has learned the secret and mysterious art of negotiation. The opponents across the table, despite their combined years of experience and superior bargaining power, don't stand a chance.

Thirty minutes later, the deal is done. The client has the greatest record deal in recent memory, the big bad record label's team are left in tatters. 'What just happened?'

they're thinking. Who is this spectacular negotiator and how had he scored such a resounding victory?

Twenty years into a career in music, this represents a pinnacle of achievement. Finally, after such an inauspicious start, he is a winner.

Except ... things didn't quite happen like that. Significant elements of the two stories are true. In the first story from the year 2000:

— Richard did accept a £6k annual salary, without question or negotiation

— His 'opponent' was a highly skilled negotiator who went on to write a bestselling negotiation book

— And sadly, yes, the end of the last century and the beginning of this one were bookended with Westlife being at number one

In the second story from 2020:

— The client in question had been at number one all summer

— The record deal that we negotiated for him was an astonishingly good one

— And it really was Richard's youngest son's favourite song, so the stakes were very high

But some of the details were embellished to fit a well-worn narrative: that through training and mastery of some mysterious techniques, anyone can go from being a negotiation loser, to a negotiation winner.

In this book, we are going to examine whether that narrative is not only false, but also particularly unhelpful.

And whether, especially in the modern economy, a 'win / lose' mindset is both outmoded, and can lead to wasted opportunities.

Let's take a look at what actually happened in these two stories.

The year 2000 salary negotiation

This story wasn't really embellished at all, but there were some important bits of information left out:

— Richard didn't mention that, prior to this interview, he had written to every single record label, music publisher and music law firm in London, to try to secure a year's work placement during his degree course.

— The interview he was attending on that day was the result of the single, solitary reply that he had received to all of those letters.

— It was his only chance — there was no plan B. If he didn't secure that job, he was going to have to start looking in other sectors for his placement year. Shipping law, maybe, or matrimonial law. There's nothing bad about either of those disciplines, but he had his heart set on music.

With hindsight, he can also see that accepting that placement was the first step in helping to build the relationships and knowhow that would set the foundations for his working life.

The salary was low, but he'd been living as a student on loans and grants for the past two years, so ... if you'd asked what his bottom line would have been in terms of an acceptable salary? It might have been even lower than £6,000. In fact, knowing now what the alternative might have been, he would probably have paid them to take him on.

Framed in this light, it doesn't feel so much like a 'lost' negotiation at all.

The 2020 record deal

Okay, cards on the table, large chunks of this one were false. It was presented in this way so that we could dispel a few myths:

MYTH 1
Negotiation has a tendency to be dramatic

We were in the middle of a pandemic, so the boardroom showdown envisaged here is pure fiction. In fact, Richard was at home in the West Country, sat at a kitchen table on a Zoom call, in the hours before the deal was signed.

There were no heroic last-minute feats of negotiation gymnastics. What happened instead was a much more prosaic chat through the intricacies of the deal, with the artist and his manager. The 'other side', the record label, didn't even feature in this conversation.

Because the real work had been done in the weeks and months before then.

MYTH 2
Winners and losers

The deal was by any measure a phenomenal result for the artist. But again, the idea that because it was a great deal for him, Richard had somehow pummelled the label into submission is false. That's because it also represented a significant victory for the label. They had succeeded in securing a long-term partnership with an extraordinary artist, and a secure platform from which to build his career, together.

Both parties were able to say with confidence that they had 'won' or, perhaps more accurately, that they had achieved the right result for them and created a positive platform for a strong future relationship.

If that wasn't the case, how could the relationship be expected to thrive in the years to come, if one side felt that they'd had it all their own way? Experience suggests that it wouldn't end well. If a negotiation like this starts lopsidedly, it's unlikely to flourish.

In this instance, everyone was going into the deal with a spring in their step, and with the foundations laid for a long-term relationship.

MYTH 3
The perfect result

The story we told you about the record deal also presents the idea that there is some kind of 'perfect' outcome in the process. A finite, black-and-white 'result'.

Again, the reality isn't quite so romantic. As we'll see later in the book, *information* is a hugely important part of the negotiation process. In any given deal, it's rare to have all of the relevant and necessary information to hand. For a start, these types of agreements often seek to look many years into the future. It would be naive to think that we can anticipate every possible event or development that is to come.

In the 1970s and '80s, arguably the heyday of rock music, many artists negotiated and renegotiated hugely lucrative recording contracts, advised by the brightest and best managers, lawyers and accountants at the time.

But how many of those agreements considered carefully what those artists would be paid when recordings of those artists' songs were magically 'streamed' on to consumers' computers and mobile phones?

The answer, it seems, is not very many. Countless disputes have cropped up in recent years from artists whose contracts imply that any such use should be treated in exactly the same way as a record sale.

So, without complete information, there can be no perfect result in a negotiation. There will always be a degree of compromise or imperfection. Let's be realistic about that.

MYTH 4
The lone wolf

Also false in this story is the portrayal of a single, skilled negotiator heroically saving the day.

As we shall see in chapter 2, our preconceptions of what makes a great negotiator (grandiose performances around a boardroom table and so on) can be unhelpful.

And, indeed, the idea that a negotiation is all about two individuals duking it out is starting to feel outmoded. While Richard was negotiating with another lawyer at the record label, the reality is that there were a lot more people involved in the process: the artist himself; their management team; the negotiation team at the record label; Richard's colleagues who put in the hours of preparation necessary to help things run smoothly; the respective families of all those involved (who throughout lockdowns and home schooling ensured there was enough headspace for them to focus on this type of complex negotiation).

Negotiation in modern business is increasingly a team sport. Making it all about you will rarely make for the best outcomes.

The heroic journey

We painted the picture of the journey from 'zero to hero'. Someone with no negotiation experience at all becomes a master of the art through grit and determination. This is a nice image. But again, it's also pretty inaccurate.

When Richard took his nine-year-old son to a Pokémon club recently and watched him trading cards with friends, it was amazing to see how innate bargaining skills seem to be hardwired into us from an early age. As social creatures, whether we realise it or not, we are constantly engaged in negotiations every day of our lives, jockeying for position, status, advantage or some other benefit for ourselves and our peers.

So, while it isn't perhaps the mysterious art that it is often portrayed as, there are subtle insights and tweaks that we can make to our own preconceptions and behaviours that will lead to *better* negotiation. Just like breathing and walking, even though it is something that comes naturally, we can strive to negotiate more consciously and mindfully.

The best negotiators we've worked with are the ones who remain curious about different approaches to bargaining (both in themselves and in others) and who work tirelessly to adapt and improve their skills.

Do Deal is a practical guide to help you along that journey, whatever stage you're at. So, shall we get started?

In business, like they say,
you don't get what you deserve,
you get what you negotiate.

Jay Z, *Decoded*

Introduction

Together we have racked up more than 50 years' experience in the music business, negotiating every day with a cast of colourful characters. In the words of Hunter S. Thompson:

> '[It] is a cruel and shallow money trench, a long plastic hallway where thieves and pimps run free, and good men die like dogs. There's also a negative side.'

It's a great quote, frequently attributed to the music business, although apparently Thompson was actually talking about the world of television ... but there are similarities. When dealing with something as ephemeral and sacred as music, it can quickly become a high-stakes game that encourages risk taking and manipulation.

In this book, we're going to look at some fascinating examples from the worlds of music, the arts and entertainment as we develop the theme of a more collaborative approach being key to better negotiation. You may not work in any of these industries, but we've tried to choose examples that will be applicable to deal-making situations across a variety of sectors. We shall also look at what to do if the person on the other side of the negotiation does not share your collaborative mindset, how to try to bring them round and win their trust — and what to do if you can't achieve this.

We believe every single negotiation is not only an opportunity to maximise transactional value, but also to deepen and enhance the relationships with the people you work most closely with, and to build and maintain mutual trust.

We sometimes have contrasting, but complementary, approaches to negotiation in our own work; this came to the fore when we were trying to work out how to write a book together! But in this short guide we shall also look at how an appreciation of the variety of different bargaining styles is another key to becoming a better negotiator.

A couple of quick disclaimers. What this book isn't:

Firstly, we're not particularly interested here with negotiating in a vacuum, that is, single-issue, one-dimensional negotiations with people you're unlikely to encounter again. While those types of negotiations do exist (haggling in a bustling marketplace on holiday with a trader you are never likely to see again), in today's hyper-connected world, negotiations like this are increasingly uncommon. Even the smallest interactions aren't without consequences — think of the rise of websites such as Tripadvisor or Trustpilot, where feedback and peer approval have become the norm in what would have previously been isolated transactions. Almost always, there's a bigger picture.

Secondly, we don't concern ourselves too much here with the resolution of disputes. Plenty has been written on these topics, and if you're unfortunate enough to find yourself in a situation where you have fallen out irreparably with someone, then we would recommend that you seek specialist advice from someone who deals with conflict resolution on a daily basis.

The type of negotiations that we are excited about exploring in this book are:

Negotiations with people who you want to build lasting relationships with. Deals that stand to benefit everybody who is involved.

The best way to get better at negotiating is to do it. But for many of us, it's something we lack confidence in, or it seems somehow mysterious. *Do Deal* will explore what negotiation is all about so you are fully prepared when the time comes. Our hope is that by the end of this book, you'll be approaching the bargaining table with greater skill and confidence, regardless of the cards you're holding. Deal?

1
Negotiation: What's the deal?

So, what is negotiation? Before we look at this question in more detail, grab a pencil, and sketch out a single simple image that springs to mind when you think of the word negotiation. What did you come up with?

A tug of war?

An arm wrestle maybe?

Perhaps it's something more convivial and optimistic, like a handshake?

Or, if you have some experience of negotiation already, then maybe the well-used metaphor of 'slicing the pie', or indeed 'growing the pie', is what sprang to mind.

A typical dictionary definition will tell you that it means: *To confer with others, in order to reach an agreement.*

That seems simple enough. So, is there a better visual metaphor for this than the ones we've just suggested?

One that we find helpful is a ball of string.

Imagine a single piece of string. In a straight-up tug of war, one side's gain will mean the other side's loss.

But in practice, most negotiations are not this one-dimensional. So, let's think instead of a tangled ball of multi-coloured string, where one party is interested in, say, blue string, whereas the other is more keen on red.

If both negotiators simply dive in and pull at the particular colour of string that they want, what might happen?

— Firstly, they're unlikely to unravel the full length of string available

— One side might get some of the red or blue string that they were after

— But they might end up having to make a compromise and cut off a small chunk when they find the rest of what they are looking for is stubbornly caught up with the remainder of the ball

It can end up becoming a tangled and frustrating business, and the practical end result is that, while each of our well-meaning negotiators has come away with a little of what they wanted, there's a huge amount of potential string (value) that has been left uncaptured. Think of all that wasted opportunity!

It's a blunt and exaggerated example, but versions of this type of negotiation are played out every day, with the parties barely communicating, meaning vast amounts of value and mutual benefit end up being left behind.

Now let's imagine an alternative scenario.

Both of our string-loving negotiators start talking to one another, not only about the type of string they favour, but also the process of *how* they might go about working together in order to get the most out of this process.

This might involve a degree of trust. Handing the end of string over to their counterpart for a moment, for instance, to allow them to untie a tricky knot; and accepting that in the process their counterpart may, for a time, look to be doing a little better out of the arrangement than they are.

But gradually, more of the string both parties are looking for starts to become freed up.

Along the way, one might discover that, as well as blue string, they also have a penchant for green string ... and their counterpart realises that they have some use for a particular type of orangey-coloured yarn.

So, while both sides have approached this particular problem with completely different priorities and interests, by sharing the common goal of unravelling this puzzle they have both:

— Ended up with more than if they'd approached it from a position of pure self-interest

— Learned a little about one another along the way

— Created a shared experience that might become the foundations of a much longer-lasting relationship

And they might even have enjoyed the interaction!

The ball of string metaphor acknowledges that the reality of most negotiations is rarely a straight-line tug of war. Invariably, there are complexities, differing needs and wants between the parties, and a strong degree of cooperation and collaboration will be essential in order to unravel those complexities, then find and distribute the most value.

To do otherwise is not only a frustrating process, it can also be extremely wasteful.

In the following chapters, we shall look at some of the techniques you can use to help extract the most value out of your negotiations, and to enrich relationships along the way.

2
What makes a great negotiator?

There's a black paperback book on the desk in front of us with bold, gold lettering all over it. A red stripe across the top of the cover reads 'Number One Bestseller'. The photo on the cover depicts a confident, coiffured man approaching retirement age, wearing an immaculate blue suit and crisp shirt cuffs with expensive-looking links. He gazes impassively at the camera, as if sizing up an opponent. In the background, blurred images of what seem to be the tops of skyscrapers imply that this man, too, is situated in the penthouse suite of a grand office building. He's at the top of his game.

A back-cover quote from the *Chicago Tribune* states that the author 'is a deal maker ... the way lions are carnivores and water is wet.' It's possibly the bestselling book on negotiation ever written. But it's probably the one you won't want to read. The book is called *The Art of the Deal*, and it's written by former US President, Donald Trump.

The cover of the book and the book itself offer an interesting insight, though, into the misconceptions of what a negotiator could, or should, look like. Tough, uncompromising, formal, uncompassionate, toxically masculine. No thanks.

While this type of negotiator still exists, and while these traits can have their place in certain kinds of modern-day negotiations, the truth is that, in the majority of our working relations, the Trump approach is outmoded and sub-optimal.

Indeed, despite how he would wish to be perceived, there are countless examples of what an appalling negotiator the 45th President of the United States probably was and is. We like this one:

When he was negotiating his part in *The Apprentice*, he concluded the deal quickly and without consulting any advisors for $50,000 per episode in the first series. After that series proved spectacularly successful, he tried to negotiate a huge pay hike.

'He wanted a million dollars an episode,' Jeff Zucker, the current boss of CNN and former head of NBC, told the *New Yorker's* David Remnick in 2017. And what did Zucker give him? 'Sixty thousand dollars,' Zucker said. 'We ended up paying him what we wanted to pay him.'

Marty Latz, the author of *The Real Trump Deal: An eye-opening look at how he really negotiates*, told Politico, 'If you take a look at the research as to the actual skills that the most effective negotiators exhibit, you're looking at skills like assertiveness, empathy, creativity, ethicality — how ethical you are — and skill sets like those are not necessarily in the DNA of Donald Trump.'

Appearances can be deceptive

When Chris Voss, former chief FBI hostage negotiator and author of *Never Split the Difference*, steps on stage to deliver one of his highly influential seminars, he doesn't immediately convey the image of a powerful negotiator that one might expect. He's more reserved, and at first reminds you more of children's author Michael Rosen than of a Trump-like city slicker. Yet he has presence, and is undeniably self-assured.

In his role as a hostage negotiator, traits like reasoning, preparation and what he terms 'tactical empathy' play a far bigger role than presenting a powerful first impression.

Thankfully, great negotiators come in all different varieties. Some of the best negotiators we've worked with are completely blasé about outward appearances. They are far more concerned with carefully analysing the components of the deal in front of them, rather than how they present themselves.

So, if the archetype of a titanium-skinned negotiator isn't fit for purpose in modern business, what does a great negotiator look like instead? Perhaps the exact opposite.

As Shakespeare wrote, 'And though she be but little, she is fierce.'

And the Dalai Lama, 'If you think you're too small to make a difference … try sleeping with a mosquito in the room.'

Not to mention Greta Thunberg whose bestseller was called, *No One is Too Small to Make a Difference.*

Being small, or inconspicuous, at the outset of a negotiation can be a big advantage. But taken too far it could mean you find yourself railroaded by your counterparts. A healthy balance is to appear calm, confident and ready to engage in the process.

We shall see later in this book that there is a time for laying your cards on the table, but it may not make sense to convey an overly strong or equally diminutive impression the moment you walk in the room, or before you have to. Neutrality in the opening stages will allow you to set the tone of the negotiation at a time and in a manner of your choosing, rather than it being apparent before you've even said a word.

Mattie Ross in *True Grit*

Movies can be great source material for observing negotiations. A favourite example of ours is a sparkling scene from the Coen Brothers' remake of the western *True Grit* that centres on Mattie Ross, an unassuming 14-year-old girl.

In the scene, Mattie bargains with a gruff old cotton trader. In order to raise funds to take a journey to avenge her father's murder, she needs to sell four ponies back to the trader that her father bought just before he was killed.

The trader gravely misjudges his negotiation counterpart. She handles the transaction almost flawlessly, and uses a number of techniques we discuss in this book, including:

— **The advantage of opening**: Mattie opens quickly and clearly, telling the trader exactly what she wants before he has a chance to ask. In doing so, she claims the opening advantage, anchoring where she wants to get to.

— **Using clear, direct and confident language**. She gives no clue that she might be nervous or underconfident and refuses to be impressed by or to acknowledge his greater experience, despite his efforts to use these factors.

— She **remains calm** and **avoids generating anger** with her counterpart; although the trader shows signs of frustration, it is because Mattie is doing better than he is.

— She has the advantage of being **completely prepared**. She has already sold cotton at a higher price, but tells him she still wants to see what price he will offer. She **keeps him in the conversation**.

— She **avoids an impasse**. When the trader initially point-blank refuses to buy back the horses, Mattie doubles down and insists he reimburses her for a saddle that was stolen. Mattie does not stop but moves the negotiation around to different points to avoid an impasse.

— She uses an **outside authority** by threatening legal action, citing her formidable lawyer who has beaten great adversaries. When the trader doubts whether she really has a case, she **reframes** it by pointing out that, in front of a jury, with a wily old trader against an orphaned child, there may be other factors involved. This is enough to get the trader negotiating properly.

— Finally, her near-perfect **preparation** covers not only her approach to the negotiation using the various points set out above, but also allows her to deal with all the points raised by the old trader.

You can find the clip on YouTube and it's well worth watching for a masterclass in a negotiation where the odds are stacked against you.

Mattie is a fictional character, of course. Let's look now at some real-life examples of negotiation prowess.

Michael and Emily Eavis

There is a wonderful real-life negotiation scene in Julien Temple's 2006 documentary *Glastonbury*, about one of the world's greatest music festivals.

The festival's founder, Michael Eavis, is confronted by a dozen or so members of the Mutoid Waste Company as the festival draws to a close. The 'Mutoids', as they're known, are a performance art group, who are famous for their giant art installations made from scrapped cars and other recycled waste. Their Wikipedia entry says they are influenced by *Mad Max* and *Judge Dredd*, so imagine the scene as they turn up on the doorstep of the Eavis family home at Worthy Farm.

Joe Rush, one of the founders of the Mutoids, has confronted Michael because he thinks they've been treated unfairly at the Festival and have been underpaid.

JOE RUSH: *This is our finale.*

MICHAEL EAVIS: (looking very concerned) *Here we go. This is really, really bad news.*

JOE: *You say we're bad news? We're the good news!*

MICHAEL: *You're so unreliable. All the way through. You invited yourselves here, I gave you 19 or however many tickets, I said we'd look after you well.*

JOE: *We gave you the best show you've had here for years. We give you the only show that isn't just —*

MICHAEL: (cutting in) *I said we'd look after you well. We've fed you for six weeks in real style. We've looked after you all the way through.*

JOE: *All your money, and a tenner in our pockets each for all the work we've put in?*

MICHAEL: *I don't know what you expected.*

JOE: *We expected to not be out of pocket.*

MICHAEL: *I've been running this show for 17 years, and I've been fair and reasonable all that time and if I hadn't been I wouldn't be here now, would I? Would I have survived 17 years if I had been a ****?*

At this point, Michael is making a very clear and powerful statement: that he's a reasonable person. By doing so, he does not threaten or create a negative reaction that makes an agreement any less easy to achieve. Michael is usually very calm, but also gives an early impression of being not easily shifted; he is no pushover.

He's not calling Joe unreasonable. We all hate it if someone does this. Our standards of reasonableness or fairness vary considerably. We all like to think we're the most reasonable people in our own little universes.

Michael's masterstroke here is to place some objective context on the situation. If he hadn't been fair and reasonable over so many years, to the enormous number of stakeholders that it takes to make an event such as Glastonbury happen … well, it simply wouldn't happen, would it?

Michael is making the point that he's not trying to short-change anyone. Joe might not accept that it's fair or reasonable from his point of view but, at this moment, behaviourally something changes. In the film, you can see a lightbulb switch. Joe understands and accepts that Michael isn't trying to rip him off, and that his hard-won reputation as an ethical person is justified.

That's the win Michael seems to be looking for here. That realisation. Because this isn't the end of the negotiation. It's not the 'Finale' that Joe alludes to at the start.

Michael is 17 years into running Glastonbury. It feels like at this point he already knows it will go on for many years to come. And that he's hoping the Mutoids will continue to be a part of that. So, the real battle here is to win the acceptance and understanding of the Mutoids that he's a reasonable man, and in fact more than fair, as that will lay the foundations for their long-term working relationship.

The interesting thing here is that Michael ends up giving Joe exactly what he asks for. It's a drop in the ocean for the festival, but it's significant for Joe and his crew.

At the end of the exchange, it's all smiles, and everyone is set for the next year. And in the final shot of the scene, we see Michael's young daughter Emily Eavis, beaming widely at all of this. 'Bye, Joe!' she grins.

It's been an entertaining meeting for her, and it's telling that as the festival now passes its 50th anniversary, with Emily joining Michael at the helm, the Mutoid Waste Company and Joe Rush remain as big a part of it as ever, a relationship that has flourished over the years.

By remaining firm, calm and not playing into the potential to create conflict, Michael has made his point. And when a concession is given, it demonstrates generosity, rather than a forced climbdown.

As we shall explore throughout this book, this idea of cultivating a reputation over time can have real benefits. Studies have shown that where a negotiator is preceded by a reputation for being uncompromising and displaying a 'winner takes all' approach, they are likely to fare worse in their dealings than a negotiator who has a reputation for being collaborative and reasonable.

Negotiators don't have to be rock stars

Many of the very best negotiators are likely people you will never have heard of. While displaying a big public persona can be advantageous in certain types of negotiations, often, as we shall see in following chapters, discretion is the better part of valour.

Richard's friend (and actually his first ever client) is an incredible musician and record producer called Dave Okumu. If you don't know Dave, you've almost certainly heard his music. He's written and produced music for the likes of Jessie Ware, Arlo Parks, Paloma Faith and Grace Jones, and he's the guy people such as Adele will call on if they want a pristine guitar lick on their record.

We have negotiated some great deals in relation to his career over the years. But the person we want to talk about here is actually Dave's dad, Professor Washington Okumu.

Richard has known Dave for nearly 20 years. However, it was only after Dave's father passed away in 2016 that he learned more about Professor Okumu's extraordinary life and legacy. Because it was Professor Okumu who, in 1994, against all odds, persuaded the South African Inkatha Freedom Party (IFP) leader Mangosuthu Buthelezi to take part in the democratic elections and, by doing so, ensured a peaceful transition for South Africa in its political journey out of apartheid.

In 1994, supporters of the two main political leaders (Buthelezi of the IFP and Nelson Mandela of the ANC) were on the brink of civil war. Top international diplomats, including Henry Kissinger and his British associate, former UK foreign secretary Lord Carrington, were making increasingly desperate attempts to halt the impending violence. There had already been clashes between the two sides in which dozens of people had been killed.

A week before the elections were due to take place, with talks at a complete impasse, the UN negotiation delegation gave up and decided to leave. On the way to the airport, Professor Okumu, who was part of the team, felt he could not just sit in silence.

In an interview with the *Independent* at the time he explains how he spelled out to Buthelezi uncomfortable truths that nobody else had seemed willing to confront him with: 'I told him that everyone, both in South Africa and the rest of the world, [said] that he would lose everything after the election and would lose any influence in future negotiations. I warned him that Nelson Mandela would not treat him kindly.'

Something in this must have chimed with Chief Buthelezi, because he wavered from his entrenched position and asked Professor Okumu to stay on, after all the other negotiators had left. Over the following days, Professor Okumu would shuttle between the leaders of the respective parties (on the jet the UN team had left behind) and broker mediation sessions that would last sometimes until 4 in the morning.

Buthelezi had been holding out for a form of federalised government, one where his party, in the parts of South Africa where it held a majority, would essentially be self-governing.

He was unmoving in this position. But Professor Okumu reportedly told him 'to think of the bigger picture and how history would treat him harshly if South Africa imploded into a slaughterhouse because of his intransigence'. At the time, the Rwandan genocide was into its second week and Professor Okumu told Buthelezi that would 'look like a picnic in comparison to a failed South Africa'.

Crucially Professor Okumu also knew both men. He had met Mandela back in the 1960s before he was imprisoned, and had known Chief Buthelezi for 20 years. By taking the time to genuinely understand what was important to the two protagonists in this negotiation, he was able to help them to find compromises that would avert catastrophe.

He persuaded Mandela to accept that the status of Zulu King would be enshrined in the South African constitution. This was a position Mandela had been reluctant to accept as he felt it would set a precedent for other chiefs and community leaders to demand similar status.

Those fears turned out to be unfounded, and Mandela's acknowledgement of Buthelezi's status went further than mere lip service. In the years that followed, in a remarkable show of conciliation, Mandela made Buthelezi acting president on 22 separate occasions when he and his deputy Thabo Mbeki were out of the country.

Professor Okumu was a quiet and reserved man, according to those who knew him. But after every single one of the UN peace negotiators had given up and gone home, he stayed the course and, through tenacity and a keen and empathetic understanding of each side's values and priorities, he was able to persuade them to see a bigger picture that was acceptable to all of them. He reframed the position for both men, depersonalising it and asking them to consider that while a certain point might be a position of principle for each of them, where would sticking to those principles lead, for their political parties, or for their country? It shifted the perspective, and that helped to shift embedded points of view. It's no exaggeration to say that, in doing so, he changed the course of history.

3
Traits: Identify and adapt your style

There is a common misconception that negotiators fall into different blunt stereotypes: the bully, the pushover, the peacemaker, etc. The reality is a bit more nuanced and human. Each of us is our own unique blend of characteristics and idiosyncrasies.

Negotiation theorists have developed various frameworks to try to identify common traits that play a role in our own negotiating style. The one that we like is by G. Richard Shell, author of *Bargaining for Advantage*. His model is in turn based on the influential Thomas-Kilmann Conflict Mode Instrument.

The Shell and Thomas-Kilmann models identify five key traits: competing, collaborating, compromising, avoiding and accommodating. These are then plotted on a two-dimensional axis. On the up/down axis, you have a scale running from 'passive' to 'assertive'. On the left/right axis, the scale runs from 'uncooperative' to 'cooperative'. Within this two-dimensional grid are plotted these five main traits that will help inform the type of negotiator we are:

— **Competing** = *Assertive × Uncooperative*
Self-confident, results-focused, tendency to pursue self-interest over mutual benefit, and in the extreme can be aggressive and/or overbearing.

— **Collaborating** = *Assertive × Cooperative*
Communicative, open, focused on finding creative solutions for mutual benefit, considers many options before deciding, and is mindful of long-term outcomes.

— **Compromising** = *as the name suggests, sits in the middle of the other four traits*
Splitting the difference, exchanging concessions, seeks a quick middle ground, results in only partial satisfaction for both parties.

— **Avoiding** = *Passive × Uncooperative*
Avoids tension or confrontation, remains objective or emotionally disconnected from their counterpart, doesn't automatically pursue their own interests or those of their counterpart.

— **Accommodating** = *Passive × Cooperative*
Focuses on maintaining a rapport and the relationship, even if that means providing greater concessions, or focusing on the needs of the other party over their own.

What's nice about Shell's test — and we would recommend you pick up a copy of his book, which contains the test in its appendices — is that rather than plonking you squarely in one or another of these categories, it scores your predispositions in each of the five traits by taking you through a series of carefully considered questions. The answers give you a 'score'. Essentially you, and every person who you negotiate with, are going to be a unique combination of these five core components.

Here's an example that highlights Richard's own results. (If you happen to be reading this ahead of a negotiation with him, that's okay, he's happy to bare his soul if it helps others to understand their own negotiation traits!)

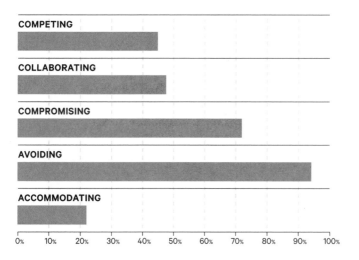

Let's look at each of those in turn and try to interpret them.

Competing
Richard scored just below the mid-point on this. Winning for winning's sake isn't something that he prioritises.

Collaborating
He's pretty much slap-bang in the middle here. In his own mind he'd love to feel he was super-collaborative, seeking creative solutions to find mutual benefit at every turn. But the test doesn't lie(!) so perhaps this is an area he needs to pay attention to if he wants to become the type of negotiator that he aspires to be.

Compromising

He's higher on this score than he would have predicted. But again, it has a ring of truth to it. The work that we do involves myriad fast-moving deals, where the priority is often to reach an agreement swiftly, and the reality dictates that, very often, compromises will need to be made.

Avoiding

When we teach our 'Music Business Negotiation' class, we find it amusing just how high Richard's 'Avoidance' score is. It's the one trait he has to contend hardest with. He grew up in a peaceful, loving family environment, but it was one in which everyone would run a mile from any kind of conflict (his wife's family are the complete opposite, so that makes for an interesting dynamic at Christmas dinner). He thinks a part of this also relates to the economy of time and energy. Anyone who is not a natural in conflict situations will attest to how draining those interactions can be. So, his learning is to not get into those situations unless absolutely necessary. The key thing to judge is recognising when it is essential to get into something head-on. And being decisive enough to commit to that course, and to commit early.

Accommodating

This is an example of how these tendencies aren't set in stone. Had Richard taken this test 20 years ago, his accommodation metric would be a lot higher. When he started working in music, he didn't really know anyone and was keen to build relationships and to be liked, and perhaps that was at the expense of focusing on the deal in hand. Today he still places a huge importance on relationships, but is far less inclined to let a desire for affirmation influence how he proceeds in a negotiation.

So, that's Richard. Warts and all.

How about you? Where would you instinctively place yourself on these scales? Can you think of a person you've dealt with recently who has displayed an abundance of one or more of these traits? Do you think your own perception of your negotiation style is aligned with how others see you?

It's important to note that for each trait no one style is more desirable than the other. We all display elements of each. We think that some of the most important keys to effective negotiation lie in:

— **Understanding** your own natural leanings and tendencies

— **Recognising** these traits in your counterparts

— **Adapting and improving** the individual elements of your negotiation style accordingly

But the *big* factor in any negotiation, the one that is going to overarch any individual negotiation trait, will be your **credibility** and **authenticity** at the bargaining table.

Seeking to adapt to a style that doesn't suit you, or that you feel deeply uncomfortable with, isn't going to get great results, and it will be exhausting. Instead, try rigorously examining your own style and leaning into any perceived weaknesses or shortcomings. Name them and work out the best way of overcoming them. For example, just because we do not lean naturally towards being competitive in a negotiation, this doesn't mean that we can't adopt a more competitive mindset when the occasion requires it.

These traits are not set in stone for any of us, and by understanding and identifying our natural tendencies and biases, we can recognise how and when we might want to adapt and modify those natural leanings, depending on the particular negotiation we are undertaking.

This does, however, reinforce the importance of preparation in negotiations to understand our own style, and where possible that of our negotiation counterpart, then to proceed accordingly.

A note of caution: Countersignalling

The traits we've just looked at may not be obviously apparent in the people you find yourself negotiating with.

Indeed, some people may go to great lengths to convey outward signals that are the complete opposite to their innermost traits or tendencies. This is known as 'countersignalling'. For example, where someone:

— is off-puttingly guileful and cunning, but chooses to present as bumbling or uninformed

— is of wealth and privilege, but chooses to ride to work on a bike, rather than in a chauffeur-driven car

— is particularly concerned about image and the impact it conveys, but might perhaps adopt a deliberately messy haircut

To say that the UK Prime Minister Boris Johnson understands and exploits the power of countersignalling would be an understatement.

Whilst we hope that all of our negotiating counterparts are straightforward and well intentioned, it's not always going to be the case. So in the early stages of your negotiations, having an understanding of the concept of countersignalling might be useful.

He who conquers others is strong;
He who conquers himself is mighty.

—

Lao Tzu

4
Key concepts: Your toolkit

There are many books on the art and skills of negotiation, each with their own take on the winning formula. This short book can't possibly cover all of those theories — and we wouldn't want to, as they don't all work!

But having spent a long time learning and applying techniques from such a wide variety of sources, there are some key concepts that — while they may seem counterintuitive at first — can help you to form the basis for any successful negotiation.

The five concepts we're going to look at are:

1. **The ZOPA** (Zone of Possible Agreement)
2. **The BATNA** (Best Alternative to a Negotiated Agreement)
3. **Framing (and reframing)**
4. **Anchoring**
5. **Normalising**

1. The Zone of Possible Agreement (ZOPA)

Every negotiation consists of one or more variables, for example, the price, the duration, or the level of exclusivity. With each of those variables, you and your negotiating counterpart will have in mind a range of outcomes between:

1. **Your best-case scenario**; and
2. **Your walk-away point** or your bottom line at the other end

The overlapping area between your range of outcomes and that of your counterpart is referred to as the Zone of Possible Agreement or 'ZOPA' (see diagram on page 68). Understanding where this zone lies should be a prerequisite ahead of any successful negotiation.

Sometimes this 'zone' won't even exist at all — your respective expectations will just be too far apart to be aligned. And it's worth finding that out sooner, rather than later.

We once worked with an artist who had been presented with a multimillion-pound record deal. We thought it was going to be the start of an intense and potentially long-winded negotiation. But when we got on a call with the artist to go through the deal and understand their priorities in relation to it, the first question they asked was: 'Will I keep the rights to my recordings?'

The simple answer was that with a record label making that level of investment, it was unthinkable that they wouldn't want to hold on to the rights in the recordings for a considerable length of time.

'Then I won't do the deal,' was the artist's position.

The money, in this instance, wasn't their key priority. Retaining their rights, and independence, was what really mattered to them.

It quickly became apparent that our expectations and the label's were very different and that, in this instance at least, we could negotiate for months and never get within the ZOPA. So, everyone decided (respecting each other's position and priorities) that it wasn't meant to be. In the words of Kellee Patterson's 1977 down-tempo disco classic, 'If it don't fit, don't force it.'

Recognising early that there isn't a zone of possible agreement can save considerable time, effort and money, by avoiding a fruitless negotiation. But those types of scenarios are fairly unusual.

In the vast majority of cases, there will be ZOPA. Sometimes it can be narrow, sometimes it can be vast. Where you start and where you end up within that zone is going to depend greatly on your understanding of and application of the other key concepts in this chapter, so let's move straight on to number two.

2. Best Alternative to a Negotiated Agreement (BATNA)

One of our maxims is NUAUAN (Never Use Acronyms Unless Absolutely Necessary): sadly, negotiation theory comes packed with them. We've tried to limit the amount we include in this book, but the BATNA *is* an essential part of your toolkit.

The Best Alternative to a Negotiated Agreement is precisely what it says on the tin: What are your options if you fail to reach agreement?

Think of it as knowing where the fire exits are when you go into a new building for the first time. If you don't have an exit route, don't be surprised if you end up getting a bit hot under the collar.

Whenever we see a negotiation go horribly wrong (by that we mean a transaction that falls apart, or that ends up very much favouring one party more than the other) a major component in this will be the fact that one side has failed to establish their BATNA; in other words, a decent alternative to the current deal.

Sometimes you won't have the luxury of a BATNA, or at least not one that you would in any real likelihood follow through with. If that is the case, it will be better to at least present the idea to your counterpart that you have a notional plan B. If they sense you have no other alternatives, you may find that you become backed into a really uncomfortable corner, or that you will be at the mercy of your counterpart, hoping they will treat you with some degree of fairness. You will not usually need to be specific about your BATNA — indeed, if you make assertions that might be checked, and thrown back at you, that could be counterproductive.

So, 'I am talking to someone else in case we can't reach an agreement,' will be preferable to 'I've received a better offer.'

The reality is that whether your BATNA is real or imagined, it will be academic once you reach an agreement.

Would the UK or the European Union have proceeded with a 'no-deal' Brexit? It's impossible to say. But crucially, both sides in that negotiation needed the other party to think that they had an alternative to a negotiated deal.

In some instances, it may be advantageous to be quite open about the fact that you have a strong sense of your own BATNA. In other instances, you might want to stay very quiet about it. But psychologically, whether your counterpart knows the details of your Plan B or not, if you know in your heart that you have other options, the confidence that gives you will mean you present yourself with greater poise and surefootedness in your dealings.

Sometimes BATNAs can be used offensively. A notable example is Rupert Murdoch's approach to moving his News International newspapers to Wapping in 1986. For years, Fleet Street, the home of newspaper publishing in the UK, had contended with poor industrial relations between the print trade unions, on the one hand, and the newspaper publishers on the other. In the early 1980s, Murdoch's news group had been seeking to impose new terms on its printers, which the print unions considered unacceptable, such as flexible working, a no-strike clause and the adoption of new technology. Historically, the unions had had the upper hand in such negotiations, because the power of industrial action in such a fast-moving industry (no printers, no papers) made bargaining with them almost impossible.

So, Murdoch's BATNA — and almost certainly his preferred outcome all along — was to secretly build a completely kitted-out new digital printing press facility in Wapping (this wouldn't rely on those union employees at all; rather than negotiating with them, he was covertly engineering a future that didn't involve them). So, when the unions made demands he wasn't happy with, Murdoch dramatically switched to his alternative plan. He got what he wanted by using his BATNA, i.e. he gave himself an alternative plan to ensure he would not be backed into a corner by the unions he was negotiating with, by circumventing them completely. It's hard to endorse such a brutal approach, but the history of Murdoch's dealings with the unions suggests that he would have been a fool not to have had a clear and deliverable BATNA, whatever you think of the morality of his actions.

The modern music industry affords artists more of an opportunity to formulate a robust BATNA than ever before. In the past, if you wanted to release a record, your routes to market were limited. You needed to work with a record label to plug into their resources, their network of marketing and promotional connections, and crucially their manufacturing and distribution supply chains.

In the 20th century, if you were an artist negotiating a record deal and your BATNA was, 'If I can't get a deal on the terms that I like, I will release the record myself', it's unlikely you would have been taken very seriously.

In today's streaming economy, self-releasing is not only possible, in many instances it is viewed by artists as the ultimate symbol of success. Artists who are bold enough to go it alone stand to benefit from a vastly increased share of the revenue that their music generates, but crucially, they will also retain the ownership of their recordings, as well as complete control over how those recordings are handled.

So today, in any serious record deal negotiation, the artist's BATNA ('We could do this without you'), looms large, and can have a significant impact on the dynamics of those discussions.

Taylor Swift's BATNA

One of the starkest examples we've seen recently of a strong BATNA in action is the widely publicised situation that pop icon Taylor Swift found herself in when someone she neither liked nor respected bought the rights to her early catalogue of albums.

For years, she had pleaded with her old record label to let her buy back the rights in her recordings. That never happened. Instead, they sold the rights in the albums in a reported $300m deal, to an investment company owned by Scooter Braun (most famous for managing artists such as Justin Bieber and Ariana Grande, and with whom Taylor did *not* get on). Taylor was incensed and publicly stated that she disapproved of the arrangement in the strongest possible terms.

But what it also meant was that the likelihood of her ever buying back those recordings herself now looked like it would never happen. She could try and negotiate with Scooter Braun but, realistically, her chances of success would be minimal.

So, what did she do instead? What was her best alternative?

She formulated an extreme BATNA by pledging to go to the drastic lengths of re-recording those early albums, meaning that two versions of those albums would then exist in the market. And when it comes to directing her army of fans to Spotify, or if a global brand wants to use one of those songs in an upcoming ad campaign, which version do we think Taylor will point them to?

These versions might not be the original, authentic recordings, but if you listen to them, they're pretty close! And the fact that they come coupled with the artist's endorsement and blessing means that, over time, their value is certain to rise. Whereas the value of the older recordings, which Swift has publicly distanced herself from, will likely diminish.

It was a drastic step, and would have cost a great deal of time and money, but it is a powerful lesson in the importance of always having a backup plan.

3. Framing (and reframing)

> Art consists of limitation. The most beautiful part of every picture is the frame.
>
> G.K. Chesterton

Framing is how we communicate a perspective on a deal that changes how the other party perceives it. When used appropriately, its effect is to legitimately influence the other party's approach and decision making.

A simple example:

One particularly persuasive and successful manager presented a folk music artist to labels. On the strength of his press shots and demo tapes (that were actually very good) he attracted very little interest within the industry.

The manager then presented the same artist in the context of his live concert footage. He was playing to a youthful and exuberant crowd who knew the lyrics and were affected by this artist's modern and engaging view of the world. The manager then went on to describe examples of other folk artists who had gone on to transcend the boundaries of that genre.

Now there was something fresh and exciting linking this artist to other multimillion-selling artists.

The labels got it. The manager had completely changed their perception of how the negotiation should play out. She had *reframed* it.

How Spotify reframed the music business

In 2010, Spotify were deep in negotiations with major record labels in America to try to allow them to use their huge catalogues of music so the company could launch in the US, making Spotify a truly global service. But at that time, the burgeoning world of digital music was effectively controlled by just one person, Steve Jobs.

Apple's iTunes had arrived at a time when the music industry needed it. He had found a way to elegantly monetise music sales, and get people back into buying music again after they had begun to abandon CDs in favour of free MP3s.

It's fair to say that Jobs *hated* Spotify. He saw the huge potential it had for disrupting Apple's fledgling à-la-carte download business model. Jobs would say, 'People want to own their music. They don't want to rent their music,' Edgar Bronfman Jr, then chairman and CEO of Warner Music Group, would recall.

That was a powerful message, and one that the established music industry was quick to adopt. For decades, they had sold records, tapes and CDs on a per-unit basis. The iTunes store was an evolution of that business model. But it wouldn't overturn it, in the way in which Spotify threatened to.

However, Jobs's view of the market, for once, wasn't quite right. It purported to know what consumers wanted, but the reality was that a generation who had, for a brief moment, tasted instant, frictionless access to all the world's recorded music via illegal file-sharing services such as Napster had no desire to go back to a pay-per-item model. The genie was out of the bottle. The toothpaste couldn't go back in the tube.

Spotify needed to change the narrative, if not for the consumers it was seeking to attract then for the major labels it needed to get on board, but who were still in thrall to Jobs and Apple. They needed to reframe it.

In an interview with the influential music industry news outlet CMU (Complete Music Update) in 2010,

Niklas Ivarsson, the top negotiator at Spotify, summed up their proposition as follows: 'Instant access, discovery and the sharing of music will be more important than ever before. If new services can develop this well, a re-engagement in music will happen where file-sharers will use legal alternatives rather than piracy.'

Let's consider this simple statement carefully. It does three things really well:

1. It shifts the focus away from the labels, and on to the consumers. But, unlike Jobs's statement, there is an acknowledgement of what people actually want, not just what the established industry wants them to want.

2. It draws attention to the future, the bigger picture.

3. It positions itself not as being radically different from the established model, but instead as a legal and convenient alternative to the real and popular threat of file-sharing sites such as Napster.

This reframing wasn't, in itself, responsible for bringing the US majors on board. There were some insanely complex and secretive negotiations that took place during the early 2010s that relied heavily on another important psychological factor, 'What's in it for me?' In this instance, the 'what' for the major labels would be a mixture of cash incentives, shares, advertising credit and what's been referred to as 'schmuck insurance' (that would ensure the labels would end up with huge payouts if Spotify sold the company within a short time-frame after securing their valuable catalogues of songs).

But we think that Ivarsson's line of thought, as quoted, was most likely the foundation that the negotiations were built on. It set the tone and got them in the room.

If they had tackled iTunes head on, suggesting they were somehow a better version of Apple's proposition, it wouldn't have had the same resonance. Although it should be noted that once people had tried the simple and seamless brilliance of Spotify's interface, and the convenience of having virtually all the world's music instantly accessible at a single click, the company's resulting dominance seemed inevitable.

Perhaps Spotify's founder Daniel Ek had been reading Richard Buckminster Fuller, the 20th-century architect and futurist who said, 'You never change things by fighting the existing reality. To change something, build a new model that makes the existing model obsolete.'

4. Anchoring

We all like to think we are highly rational and objective. But in reality, our viewpoint and behaviour can be affected by seemingly unconnected factors or information.

Daniel Kahneman's bestselling book *Thinking Fast and Slow* explores some of these ideas brilliantly. In one example, he describes an experiment carried out with his long-time collaborator Amos Tversky.

It combined a roulette wheel with a tricky question. Each participant rolled a ball on to a roulette wheel, that, unknown to them, was rigged so that the ball would only land on the number 10 or 65. They were then asked to respond to a completely unrelated question: 'What percentage of UN members are African nations?'

The results of the experiment were illuminating. For those whose number on the wheel landed on 10, the average guess was a 25 per cent membership. Those who landed on 65, however, answered the same question, with a much higher number of 45 per cent.[1]

So why were smart, intelligent people being influenced by something as arbitrary as the last number they saw? There's certainly no actual relationship between the number on the wheel and UN membership percentage.

The answer can be found in the concept of **anchoring** that plays an unseen role in our everyday lives, and that is pivotal in understanding how to negotiate better.

Anchoring is a cognitive bias in which the brain will tend to fixate on the first, or most dominant, factor that it is presented with, and then (usually unconsciously) we lopsidedly base our perceptions and negotiation around that initial starting point.

Our brains like to build a simplified picture of what is happening in any given situation. It allows us to draw conclusions and react more quickly. Some elements in these mental pictures will be more dominant than others. For our primitive ancestors, it might have been a snake lurking in the grass spotted out of the corner of their eye. Today, it could be the click-bait headline that you are drawn to while scrolling through social media.

The type of modern business deals that we negotiate are invariably complex and multifaceted. But if you asked 100 people to name one thing that might be important in a record deal, for example, we bet most of them (even those with no experience of the industry) would probably answer: 'The Advance.'

The Advance. It's very glamorous-sounding. Aspiring pop stars dream of it, the tabloid press have a lurid fixation on it. Rappers dedicate verses to the size of it.

The Advance is precisely what the name suggests. It's a prepayment of future earnings. It might take your

---

1   The actual answer is 28 per cent (54 of the 193 members as at 2020)

music five years to earn £1,000,000 in royalties. So if a record label or song publisher offers you an advance of £900,000 today, that's going to grab your attention.

There are many other factors that the company could focus on to try to entice you, of course:

— The investment the company might make in marketing and promoting your music

— The cachet of working with a particular label

— Or just having a team of great people around you

But it's easy to see how each of those things can melt into the background when set against one big, bold number. That's an anchor.

As it's such a powerful and persuasive tool, we shall take a closer look at the application of anchoring and the impact of placing these strong, unambiguous markers down in the early stages of negotiations in more detail in chapter 7.

5. Normalising

In James Clear's influential 2018 book *Atomic Habits* he states, 'We imitate the habits of three groups in particular: The close. The many. The powerful.'

By *'the close'* he means those nearest to us, our family and inner circle of friends or colleagues.

By *'the many'* he means our wider tribe, the societal groups with whom we identify.

By *'the powerful'* he means that we are influenced by those who we perceive to have a high status, or whom we aspire to emulate.

The focus of his book is the power of habits, but the subconscious behavioural patterns we see in the formation of habits also play an important role when we negotiate.

Both we and our counterparts are instinctively drawn to positions that would be considered acceptable by our peers: 'What would normally happen in this situation?' When coupled with framing and anchoring, understanding the power of these norms can be important in understanding what your counterpart's position might look like, and it will often help steer things towards an acceptable outcome.

We see this all of the time in record deals. The terms of the deal can vary enormously, and in isolation it can be difficult for an artist to gauge what is objectively fair or reasonable. The type of question that we get asked a lot by Client A will be: 'What did Client B get in their deal?'

Rightly or wrongly, people rarely take absolute positions on points in a negotiation. Instead, experience would suggest that those positions are often relative: relative to our peers, and relative to the norms of the situation or sector that we operate in.

Consider this the other way around. If your counterpart is taking an extreme or unusual position, what could you say or demonstrate in order to place that position into a context that contrasts it to the relative norms?

Could you highlight the position of one of the groups that James Clear describes?

— A position that a colleague of theirs has taken? (*The close*)

— The position that most of the other players in their category would take? (*The many*)

— An example of a stance that the leader in their field would take? (*The powerful*)

It's likely that one or more of these examples will resonate with your counterpart. So in the Michael Eavis example that we gave in chapter 2, he was effectively saying to Joe Rush: I've been doing this for years, everyone involved with this festival *(the many)* knows me to be a fair and reasonable person, can't you see that too? In other words, he normalised his response within the negotiation.

Summary

1. **The ZOPA (Zone of Possible Agreement):** Consider your best position and your walk-away point, and try to anticipate what those might look like for your counterpart too.

2. **The BATNA (Best Alternative to a Negotiated Agreement):** Consider the metaphor of the fire exit. If things aren't working out as you'd like them to, do you have another option and a clear route out?

3. **Framing:** Think about the wider context of your negotiation. Aside from the nuts and bolts of the deal you're about to discuss, think about the ultimate objectives you're both seeking to accomplish.

4. **Anchoring:** Use clear anchors when you start your negotiation. If your counterpart gets there first, think about how you can identify and diffuse their anchors.

5. **Normalising:** What's the right thing to do? It's such a subjective question. So try to relate that question to groups of like-minded people, and how they may have approached similar situations in the past.

5
Process: Lay your foundations

We often think we are fortunate working in the music business because most negotiations follow a clear process that goes something like this:

1. **Initial interest:** Two parties (let's say a record label and an artist) decide they want to work together.

2. **Opening:** One side makes an offer to the other (usually the record label or the party acquiring rights from the other — but this isn't always the case, as we shall see in chapter 7). That offer will tend to be an email or a single sheet of paper, a memorandum of the main deal points, often referred to simply as the 'Deal Memo'.

3. **Negotiate the 'Deal Memo':** Both parties and their respective advisors (lawyers, managers etc.) negotiate back and forth on the main deal points (the advance, the royalty, the length of the deal, the extent of the rights being granted etc.).

4. **Deal points agreed:** Once there is a consensus on the deal terms, there is usually an understanding that the parties have a 'deal'. Normally, if the artist had been simultaneously negotiating with any other labels up until this point, then those competitors would be told

at this stage that they were not going through to the final stages.

5. **Negotiate the longform agreement:** While it's tempting to think the deal is done at stage 4, the reality is that the 'devil is in the detail' and that a more fleshed-out contract is almost always advisable. This will deal with the many different mechanisms and safeguards that ensure that, should things not work out as planned, both parties have some clarity as to their respective rights and obligations.

6. **Signing:** Once everything has been negotiated and agreed, the deal is signed and the parties are committed to working together.

Devil in the detail

In the TV show *Dragons' Den*, we get to see steps 1 to 4 play out in front of us.

A contestant walks into the room, presents their pitch, makes their opening offer, and then there is a short negotiation that revolves around how much cash they will get in exchange for what share of equity, with perhaps one or two juicy conditions thrown in. This is followed by a handshake and, we're led to believe, a 'done deal'.

The reality is much different, of course. After the show there is a lengthy negotiation of the details of the investment and a due-diligence process where the contestants' claims are scrutinised. In many instances, the 'deal' may not get fully consummated and signed.

So, while it's tempting in our fast-moving world to focus on the headline points, it's helpful to work on the basis that 'nothing is agreed until everything is agreed'.

The details are vitally important. They will ensure that once an agreement is reached there is a clear and unambiguous framework around the relationship and, most importantly, that the deal itself can actually be implemented over time. For instance, what's the use in saying how much someone will be paid unless it also states clearly when and how those payments will be made?

A careful and studied approach to these later stages of the negotiation is important, as it helps you and your negotiation counterpart to get to know and respect what is important to each of you. It shows you care about not just the surface level of the relationship that you're building, but also the underlying nitty-gritty of it.

In the fifth verse of Henry Wadsworth Longfellow's poem *The Builders*, he highlights the fact that in ancient monasteries you will find beautifully crafted woodwork and masonry high up in the roof or tucked away behind the beams where nobody is ever likely to see it:

> In the elder days of Art,
> Builders wrought with greatest care
> Each minute and unseen part;
> For the Gods see everywhere.

For another more rock'n'roll example, let's look at the band Van Halen's notorious 'no brown M&M's' rider request.

It was a seemingly ludicrous request, but it was there for a very good reason. They had an extremely complex technical rider that specified the ins and outs of the sound and light set-up. If they arrived at the venue and found a bowl of M&M's that still had the brown ones in it, they knew they would need to check the sound and lighting rig very carefully, because someone hadn't read the rider diligently enough.

Agree a process

The subject matter of the agreements that we negotiate every day varies enormously. But the process will usually follow the six stages highlighted earlier. The stages themselves may vary in duration or complexity, but it's a fairly consistent linear process that we can rely on as a framework for getting deals done.

Of course, some scenarios will be brand new. There won't be a fixed process or a road map on how to proceed. These negotiations can often be really challenging. Not only do you need to reach an agreement on the substance, or the 'what', of your negotiation, you also need to try to work out the 'how', 'when', 'where', 'why' and 'who' of it.

By diving straight into the haggling over the deal points, it can feel like both sides are working against each other from the outset — which rarely makes for the best outcomes.

An extremely useful technique, when approaching a negotiation that covers new ground for you and your counterpart, is to start out by agreeing on the process, before you even begin to debate the *substance* of the deal.

Examples of parts of the process that you could focus on initially might include:

— Identifying the main points you want to reach agreement on before going any further

— The timeframe for reaching a consensus on those initial steps

— Where the negotiations will take place

— Who will be involved at each stage of the deal (when will you hand over to lawyers etc.)

— Rules-of-the-road: how you will each conduct yourselves, acceptable standards of behaviour etc.

— Protocols for ending the negotiations if they aren't proving fruitful (remember your BATNA from chapter 4)

These types of points can prove difficult. In something as high-level as the negotiation of a peace treaty between countries, things like *where* the discussions will take place will often in themselves be thorny issues.

But generally, these practical and procedural steps will be a lot simpler to reach agreement on than the substantive issues of the deal itself. By starting off with agreeing on these practicalities, you're both getting into a mindset of consensus and agreement. You've worked out how to agree on things together; even if those things aren't the crux of the matter, you can feel more comfortable about getting to those in due course. This is the warm-up.

In this warm-up, you're also going to have a chance to build a rapport with your counterpart and get to know them. You'll start to get a sense of what's important to them. Discover what kind of negotiator they are and allow them to develop trust and understanding in you — as you display a degree of openness and professionalism in these preliminary discussions.

Concede small points at the outset, give and take easy wins where you can and, before you know it, you're in the zone of a collaborative and beneficial relationship.

6
Preparation is everything

As we've seen, before we get started on the deal itself we want to get into the practicalities. Who, what, why, where, when and how questions will all help.

Consider the stages of the process that the negotiation will follow that we looked at in the preceding chapter. How long do you think this process will take? Is there a deadline for completion?

Also, consider who will be conducting the negotiation: will you and your counterpart have the full authority to negotiate and conclude the deal between you? This is surprisingly rare, as usually one side or the other will need to go back to a colleague, an investor, a client or a principal during the negotiation, to take instructions and establish exactly what they can or can't agree to. Try to get a sense of how those relationships are likely to work, both on your side of the table and your counterpart's. It is important that you understand your counterpart's level of authority, and they know you understand it as well.

What type of negotiator are you dealing with? We looked at some of the differing personality types you might encounter in chapter 3, and later in the book we shall examine some of the trickier characters you might encounter.

Have you worked with this person before? Do you know someone who has worked with them? How did that play out? What can you learn from those previous interactions?

Understanding your position

A crucial aspect of preparing for any negotiation involves taking a closer look at the two acronyms that we introduced in chapter 4: ZOPA and BATNA.

We can visualise them as follows:

We can see that we have our zone. Our counterpart has their zone. And there is hopefully an overlap in the middle where we can reach an agreement.

So, how do we go about establishing the thresholds for each of these positions?

It's simple enough to say that we should consider our best-case and worst-case positions, but in practice this is where a lot of us come unstuck. Am I asking for too much? Or not enough? What would be reasonable in this situation? What would be fanciful?

The answers to these questions will of course be highly subjective and vary, not only from situation to situation, but also between different negotiators.

In chapter 3 we looked at the five different negotiation styles. Your own cocktail of those traits is likely to dictate how you assess where you pitch your negotiation.

Homework

The simple and obvious, but often overlooked, way to prepare for a negotiation is to gather as much relevant information as possible before even beginning to consider how you will approach the bargaining table. Such information might include what you can reasonably expect in terms of the deal itself (and will help you to establish your ZOPA and BATNA), such as:

— Price

— Duration of the deal

— Exclusivity of the deal

— Payment terms

— Rights and obligations

But it may also include information about the people you are negotiating with:

— What kind of negotiator are they?

— Do they call the shots in the negotiation, or will they need to go back and check with their boss?

— How important is this deal to them compared to the other projects they are currently involved with?

If the deal you're preparing for is covering new ground, or new to you, then you're likely to instinctively do your homework. But as negotiations become more routine, it's often easy to bypass this stage. You shouldn't.

The author Malcolm Gladwell popularised the idea of the 'Maven' (the kind of people who have an insatiable curiosity and who are highly skilled in both gathering and retaining information).

Richard grew up in a small village in Devon. When he was about nine years old, a new family moved in down the road. Two brothers: Jono (a year younger than Richard) and James (a couple of years older). Both were hugely into music, and Richard's friendship with Jono is what led to his lifelong passion and work in this area too. Jono helped him to choose and save up for his first synthesiser (he now has far too many synthesisers).

But what he didn't know at the time is that both brothers were natural-born *mavens*.

When it came to music, or sport or video games, they wanted to know *everything*. And they were super-resourceful about how they went about finding things out. In a time before the internet or eBay, Jono, aged eight, was reading the classified ads top to bottom, looking for a musical instrument that might have been wrongly listed, or simply to get an understanding of the range of value that a particular item might sell for.

When it came to buying that first keyboard, he knew exactly what he wanted to pay, and got it for a great price.

As he got a bit older, he mastered the more difficult (but lucrative) skill of selling at the right price. If he were selling a guitar or a drum machine, he would sometimes place a 'dry-run' ad in the classifieds at perhaps an unrealistically high price, to see what offers might come in, and then withdraw the ad before placing another, armed with his market research, at a price he knew he could get, and would stick to.

Whenever we bump into James at a meeting or a music industry conference, he's lost none of his maven-like zeal and will still seek out and soak up information like a sponge. He has the ability to charismatically glean all sorts of details out of you. People can be particularly coy when it comes to finding out about the price of a given thing. But James will give a sincere and beaming smile and ask innocently: 'How much does one of those go for these days?'

It's worth noting that Jono and James's approach to negotiation has paid off. They have founded and run one of the most successful independent electronic music labels in the world, Anjunabeats.com, and Jono, as part of his group Above & Beyond, has some of the following achievements under his belt: multiple Grammy award nominations; top-five rankings in the annual global Top 100 DJs poll for four years in a row; and sell-out global tours, including as the first British DJs to headline Madison Square Garden.

Jono also still somehow finds time to help Richard to research and buy synthesisers, a topic that he remains endlessly curious about.

So, don't be shy about asking for information that could help inform your position. Be resourceful and creative in doing so. If you ask nicely, you'll be amazed what people will tell you. Just be sure to interpret it carefully in order to gain the full benefit of the information they share with you.

Aspirations vs expectations

In chapter 4 we looked at the ZOPA (Zone of Possible Agreement). You'll recall that ZOPA was defined by our walk-away points at one end, and our best-case scenarios at the other.

A more common term for that best-case position would be our 'aspiration'.

At the other end, what do we take as a given? What simply has to figure in this deal in order for it to happen; that's our 'expectation'.

If you book a hotel, there's an *aspiration* that the room might have a balcony, or a sea view.

There's an *expectation* that the sheets will be clean, and that you'll have hot and cold running water.

These two boundaries are set by your own standards. And they will go on to dictate where you start out in any given negotiation, and where you end up.

You may have unrealistic expectations, or aspirations. You may end up disappointed time and again, but by raising the bar of these aspirations and expectations, you may, over time, start to find you are achieving the results you want.

When looking for an example of the power of aspiration/ expectation in negotiation (and more generally), we think of our friend and former colleague, Richard Antwi, who tragically died in 2016, aged only 38.

What will have struck anyone who negotiated with Antwi was how high he set the bar in terms of expectations and aspirations. In doing so, he continually moved the zone of what was possible for the artists and businesses who he worked with, in a positive direction.

Antwi's friends and family decided that they would honour his outlook and legacy by establishing the Richard Antwi Scholarship. This champions Black, Asian and

Minority Ethnic aspiring music business professionals. Supported by all three major UK record labels (Sony, Universal and Warner), music publishers, and several of the top independent music companies and music law firms, the scholarship continues Richard Antwi's legacy of supporting young people with talent and ambition.

Our mutual friend Matt Ross describes Antwi as follows on the scholarship's website:

> Richard was a much-loved and widely respected music manager, lawyer and entrepreneur. Always ahead of the curve with sharp instincts, great ears and a handsome smile. As Carl Fysh succinctly put it, Richard was quietly at the centre of everything.
>
> Of Ghanaian lineage, Richard's story was written in Wembley, progressing from a state comprehensive to study law at the University of Oxford, before embarking on a successful career that saw him play pivotal roles in the ascendance of many of the artists and executives currently making moves and running major matters in the UK.
>
> The breadth of Richard's support for others became abundantly clear when he passed so suddenly in 2016. The affection and respect in which he was held by so many people across the music industry and beyond, manifested in a desire to channel this goodwill and emotion in a way that captured his legacy and found a way to continue it.

We've been fortunate enough to have had a number of the graduates from the scholarship join us on our 'Music Business Negotiation' courses. In the second week, we run a simple exercise that touches on the ideas that we've highlighted over the past few chapters. It involves a simple record deal and setting a suitable BATNA and ZOPA in preparation for that negotiation. The courses typically attract a wide cross-section of individuals from across the music business. Lawyers from indie and major record labels, managers of platinum-selling artists, 'old hands' looking to sharpen up their skills.

So we were delighted, when it came to analysing the results of this particular exercise, to see that it was Daniel, one of the graduates from the Richard Antwi Scholarship, who had set their expectations and aspirations markedly higher than any other participant on the course.

Look at what that means in the context of the diagram on page 68. The ZOPA was shifted in his direction, and a more favourable result was assured.

Events of recent years have shown us that the music industry, as well as virtually every other part of society, has a worryingly long way to go in terms of issues of diversity and inclusion. While those changes may not happen overnight, we believe strongly that Antwi's approach of consciously and consistently raising expectations and aspirations has a vital role to play in effecting lasting positive change.

Let us never negotiate out of fear.
But let us never fear to negotiate.

John F. Kennedy

7

Opening the deal: 'After you', 'No, I insist, after you!'

There is a perceived British tendency to politely sit back and let others come to you with their best offer. While this can sometimes be a useful approach, in this chapter we shall look again at the concepts of anchoring and framing to illustrate why, often, it pays to set the pace and put your best foot forward.

In many of the deals we negotiate, the 'buyer', i.e. the side that is acquiring the rights (in music deals this is usually the record label or the song publisher), will start the negotiations by making the first offer.

The side whose rights are being acquired, the 'seller' (in this example, the artist), will usually wait for the offer or offers (sometimes musicians can find themselves in a 'bidding war') to come in and then negotiate from there.

But let's look at this in the context of anchoring from chapter 4.

The relationship between the buyers and sellers in this type of transaction is already quite asymmetrical: in other words, they may have unequal status or power.

The record label usually has considerably more information (prior deals, market trends and, more recently, reams of data and analytics) and resources (funding, staff, knowhow etc.) than the artist. An inexperienced artist can seek to redress this imbalance by hiring a smart manager or a flashy lawyer, but costs can quickly escalate.

A crucial advantage the label might have is that they've done a *lot* of these types of deals before. And, consciously or unconsciously, they will be aware that by putting an offer in first, and by focusing attention on an eye-catching advance, then this negotiation, like the one before that, and the one before that, is more likely to go their way.

Remember our example from chapter 4, the artist who was presented with a multimillion pound record deal? Once the big attention-grabbing number is lodged in someone's mind, it can be hard to shift.

It's also worth noting that anchoring around the advance is a very smart move for the label. Because even if it's a huge number, that advance is still a prepayment of the artist's future earnings. So, if things go as well as everyone hopes, the size of the advance won't have been a factor for a well-funded label. (That's *if* things go well. The other side, of course, is that many artists never recoup those big advances, so in that sense there is a real risk for labels when assessing the level of advance).

A negotiation built around a healthy advance is pure anchoring.

But what if we flip the script?

What would it look like if the seller (artist) had anchored first, and early? How would the buyer (label) react?

Andrew experienced this scenario when he was the senior lawyer at a large record company. A label CEO and Andrew met with an experienced manager who had recently started to represent a very well-known artist, with consistent high earnings over many years.

After a very brief exchange, he surprised them by immediately opening with, 'We are looking for an advance of one million pounds.' Andrew nearly fell off his chair.

It wasn't worth that much and definitely not what he had discussed with the label CEO. This opener was followed by a few weeks of intense negotiations.

But, to cut a long story short, the manager got his million-pound advance. From the moment he gave the number, the buyer was thinking of *how* he could get to pay that advance. Imagine how different it would have been if the manager had opened by asking what the best offer was? It's likely that half that amount would have been offered, ideally paid in instalments and with conditions imposed. The manager had anchored early, and grabbed the advantage of opening.

Of course, the artist in this instance was already extremely successful and had a significant degree of bargaining power at their disposal. Anyone at the early stages of their career won't normally have that luxury. But whatever the perceived power balance in a negotiation, understanding the principles of opening and anchoring can play a huge part in redressing that power dynamic.

Studies in this area are clear. Anchoring plays an undeniable role in the outcome of almost any negotiation.

Clear, concise, confident

When you open and when you anchor, ensure your language is clear and concise. Extra words will suggest a lack of confidence in your position. If you've prepared well, you can speak plainly about what you want.

At this early stage in the negotiations, it shouldn't be necessary to justify or explain why you have come up with this proposal. It is what it is. As the negotiation proceeds, the discussion may open up around specific points. But at the outset, when you open or when you respond to an opening offer, be bold and unambiguous.

Simply listing your expectations as bullet points is often all that's needed. We often see lengthy emails justifying each point. But what do we all do instinctively when we receive emails like this? We skip to the bottom line anyway.

The anchor is a simple and strong visual metaphor. That's why it works!

What happens if you can't open?

Sometimes the other party gets in first. However, there is nothing to stop you giving an early indication of what you are thinking, to manage expectations. If you are hit with that first demand, if your counterpart drops a big old anchor right on your front lawn, a useful tactic to dealing with it (and to dealing with difficulties in negotiations generally, as we come to in chapter 9) will be to:

Step 1: **Identify it**. If someone has placed a big arbitrary number down in the opening stages, it's helpful to see it for what it is: an anchor.

Step 2: **Diffuse it.** You can start the expectation-management process immediately. 'Having looked at the figures, we were thinking of something more like half that amount.' Or, 'That's a pretty high number and I don't think we can pay that much.'

What you have done is to put into the other side's head a different idea or a number. Do not say, 'We'll think about it,' or simply, 'I'll check,' because those phrases do not shift the other side's expectation in any way. Whatever you do, use simple, clear wording.

Diplomacy is the art
of letting someone else
have your way.

———

Sir David Frost

8
Collaboration

Whatever we might think of it, the television series *Love Island* has become something of a cultural phenomenon in recent years. But what does this programme have in common with:

— The comedian Jasper Carrott[2]

— The former daytime talk-show host Robert Kilroy-Silk

— Two gang members in prison cells awaiting charge

If you're familiar with game theory, you may have spotted the clue in the last point.

The climax of each season of *Love Island* ends with an exercise that is virtually identical to the final round of Jasper Carrott's game show *Golden Balls*, and that mirrors the entire premise of Robert Kilroy-Silk's ill-fated and awfully named game show *Shafted*.

The exercise is known as the 'Prisoner's Dilemma'. In its simplest form, it highlights why two completely rational negotiation counterparts may not always collaborate, even when it is in their best interests to do so. It goes something like this:

Two gang members are arrested. Each is put in a separate cell, with no way of communicating with each other. The authorities don't have sufficient evidence to convict the pair on the more serious charge. But they do have enough to convict them of a less serious offence. The arresting officers give each prisoner one of two choices: they can betray the other prisoner by testifying that the other committed the crime; or they can cooperate with the other prisoner by remaining silent.

The four possible results in this game are:

1. If prisoners A and B each betray the other, each of them serves two years in prison

2. If A betrays B but B remains silent, A will be set free and B will serve three years in prison

3. If A remains silent but B betrays A, A will serve three years in prison and B will be set free

4. If A and B both remain silent, both of them will serve only one year in prison on the lesser charge

This 'payoff matrix' can be summarised and presented as follows:

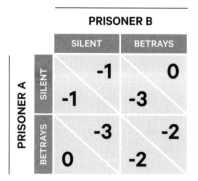

		PRISONER B	
		SILENT	BETRAYS
PRISONER A	SILENT	-1 / -1	0 / -3
	BETRAYS	-3 / 0	-2 / -2

When set out as starkly as this, it seems obvious that a purely rational and self-interested convict, would betray their mate, as that will yield the greatest reward for themself.

But follow this through and it would mean that the only possible outcome for two such rational individuals would be for them both to betray the other, even though the other option (to tactically cooperate with each other by remaining silent) would result in a best-case, or in this instance 'least worst-case' outcome overall.

Let's think impartially about this.

The net yield in the cooperation scenario means that the overall jail time in that scenario is a measly two years in total between the two. Only two Christmases where two sets of kids won't see their parents (one Christmas each). The aggregate level of misery in this scenario seems minimal.

In the betrayal scenarios, where just one informs on the other, someone's family isn't going to see them for three whole years.

And in the 'mutually assured destruction' option, where both parties snitch on each other, they both end up spending two years away from home.

In reality, and in the extensive experimental research in this area, it has been demonstrated that humans have a tendency towards cooperative behaviour in these types of gameplay exercises despite what an algorithm might predict when considering how rational, purely self-interested individuals might act.

Love Island is a show in which young people compete to couple up and find a perfect love match, within the confines of a luxury Mediterranean villa. It's very popular. In the final episode of each series, the winning couple play a version of the 'Prisoner's Dilemma' game.

The couple who have received the biggest popular vote are asked whether they want to choose love or money (as opposed to the prisoner's dilemma of 'stay silent' or 'betray').

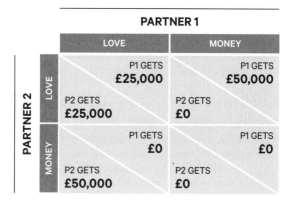

PARTNER 1

		LOVE	MONEY
PARTNER 2	**LOVE**	P1 GETS **£25,000** / P2 GETS **£25,000**	P1 GETS **£50,000** / P2 GETS **£0**
	MONEY	P1 GETS **£0** / P2 GETS **£50,000**	P1 GETS **£0** / P2 GETS **£0**

If both contestants choose love, the £50,000 cash prize is split equally between them. If one of them chooses money whereas the other chooses love, the contestant who chose money gets the full £50,000.

But if they *both* choose money, they each get nothing.

Not very romantic, is it?

Perhaps surprisingly, over the numerous series, the finalists seem to invariably both choose the love option and split the money.

The optimist in us says that this is because their true love has prevailed. The slightly cynical entertainment lawyer in us says that they will both have been made aware of how much more lucrative the spin-off TV shows, endorsement deals and sponsorship will be for a happy and in-love pair than for a couple where one partner has completely abused the trust of the other!

The dynamic in Jasper Carrott's game show *Golden Balls* is slightly different.

Again, there's a variation of the 'Prisoner's Dilemma' game in the final round. But in that show, the contestants aren't likely to have any ongoing relationship with one another. And so, the trust dynamic is different.

In fact, everything in the show that precedes the final round tends to be used by the wilier contestants as an opportunity to build trust with their counterparts, before pulling the rug out from under them at the last moment and exploiting that trust.

Earning trust before exploiting it is sometimes thought of as a useful negotiation tool. But in today's hyperconnected world, it's likely that such techniques have less value (again, think about Tripadvisor). Whether people recognise it or not, short-term interactions may now have longer-term reputational consequences.

The music business is a microcosm of this. It remains a relatively small industry. It is incredibly interconnected. Someone who starts as an artist may quickly go on to run a label of their own, which in turn may become absorbed by a major record label. The tables get turned quite quickly, and someone who was once asking a favour of you might very quickly become someone who you are beholden to or holds a grudge against you.

When we play the 'Prisoner's Dilemma' game on our 'Music Business Negotiation' course, we play it over a number of rounds. When one side chooses to 'exploit' the other early, it can taint the whole nature of the exercise: neither side trusts the other, and winning that trust back can become almost impossible. It is an interesting example of where creating trust or mutual understanding at an early stage in a negotiation can set both sides up for the best possible shared result.

We raise the stakes as we go along, so in some games both teams will display a lot of trust in the early stages, but as the game progresses and reaches the later rounds, the temptation to act with self-interest starts to ratchet up too.

In the music business — and undoubtedly in many other industries and walks of life — we find ourselves collaborating with the same groups of people again and again. So, in this sense, our negotiations become akin to a very long and slightly more complex version of the 'Prisoner's Dilemma' game, played over many, many rounds.

When we're establishing trust, we're not suggesting that we should lay all of our cards on the table at the very outset of the negotiation. Instead, a graceful dance or an interplay of uncovering and sharing information piece by piece is usually considered the best approach.

Sometimes making a concession or a disclosure early on — as long as it's one that does not undermine your negotiating position — may just gain you an advantage.

Here's an example of a tactical disclosure. Doing a record deal for a hot young recording artist, the artist needed to move to a new studio that was great value, perfectly situated and a good price. There was a deadline for offers so he needed to finalise a record deal by a certain date and release the advance. Some would argue this background information should not be disclosed. However, as a lever to encourage the label to complete by a certain date, this detail was both critical and helpful. We made sure they knew that there were other interested parties, without creating an auction or using it as a threat. It also allowed our contact at the label to tell her boss why they needed to decide immediately or lose the deal. It created momentum without increasing the risk. Ultimately, we did the deal in time and the artist secured the studio.

It's also worth remembering that all negotiation is a form of collaboration, and sometimes sharing your reasoning in this way can help move things along!

2   The unassuming comic from the Midlands may himself be a great negotiator it seems. Jasper Carrott was an early-stage investor in Celador, the production company that went on to develop one of the biggest TV show formats of all time *Who Wants to Be a Millionaire*. It's unclear how much he invested initially, but a 2006 Guardian article reported that when the company was sold to a Dutch media firm, Carrott and his wife netted more than £10 million.

9
Overcoming difficulties

Marcus Aurelius knew a thing or two about overcoming difficulties, presiding over a particularly troubled time for the Roman empire. His collection of stoic maxims *Meditations* is essential bedtime reading for any aspiring negotiator. We could pick any one of dozens of quotes from his writings to illustrate the importance of recognising and overcoming obstacles, but settled on this one:

> The impediment to action advances action.
> What stands in the way becomes the way.

Most negotiations will generate some tricky moments and hard-to-solve problems. The moment you think it is going smoothly, an obstacle will invariably present itself. Difficulties are definitely part of the adventure. Fixing them is much more satisfying than nothing ever going wrong. If nothing ever goes wrong, then you are probably not trying or pushing hard enough.

If we come across a difficult situation, we try to identify it, or even give it a name. In the cold light of day, it becomes less troublesome and, better still, you can work out how to go about fixing it. By identifying and naming these difficulties, you also build up a playbook over time of how to spot and resolve the hurdles that crop up again and again in negotiations.

We've picked out nine extremely common setbacks, named them, sketched out how we might identify them and suggested tactics for dealing with them.

1. **The Overwhelmer**
2. **Impasse**
3. **Ultimatum**
4. **Moving the goalposts**
5. **Is there anybody out there?**
6. **Boredom**
7. **Let me check with my boss**
8. **Backseat negotiators**
9. **Mistake paralysis**

1. The Overwhelmer

Throughout this book, we encourage collaborative negotiations, because we believe they create more value and better relationships in the long term.

But many people you encounter won't adopt the same approach. There are still lots of win/lose negotiators — 'distributive' is the technical term. And these types of negotiators often seek to win by *overwhelming*. This doesn't mean we should abandon a collaborative approach when dealing with such people, but we may need to adapt accordingly.

Overwhelmers come in many forms. Some of the techniques you might encounter include:

— Talking fast
— Patronising behaviour

— Claiming greater experience or intellect
— Playing hardball
— Feigning lack of commitment to the deal
— Aggression

In the early stages of a negotiation, try to identify if you are dealing with an Overwhelmer and, if so, adopt a strategy for dealing with them. This might include:

— Slowing them down: on a call or in a meeting, summarise their position back to them. If they've bombarded you with information, dissect that, pick out the bones and restate the position to them unambiguously. Seek confirmation from them that your understanding is correct.

— If they are suggesting you don't understand something, don't accept this. You have a right to understand, they have an obligation to be clear. Telling someone they don't understand is a con-artist technique. Say you need their argument to be clear in order to discuss it with colleagues.

— If they have feigned a lack of interest — 'We can take or leave your deal' — take this with a pinch of salt. They are in the negotiation for a reason. Propose a completion deadline to test their interest. Use your ZOPA and BATNA to remind yourself of your parameters.

2. Impasse

If the deal seems to be hitting a brick wall, try to stay fluid and positive. If a specific point is not agreed, move on. Look for common ground elsewhere, however minor. This will help to maintain forward momentum and energy.

Never make one term a condition of continuing or setting a red line. The phrase 'deal breaker' gets used a lot, but it's not recommended unless you are 100 per cent committed to it. As the legendary music manager Jazz Summers once quipped to a contemporary of ours: 'Don't they teach you English at Legal School? Deal breaker means deal breaker, not f***ing "send me another email".'

Use carefully considered questions to unpack what appears to be a dead end, i.e. questions that give your counterpart the opportunity to think through and solve a negotiation problem themselves. For instance: 'How can we get this back on track?'

3. Ultimatum

As with the deal breaker example above, we'd advise against giving ultimatums. If one is given to you, the best advice is to politely ignore it. Expressions like 'red lines' or 'final offer' can lead back to an impasse and annoy the other side.

What you really want, at some point, is for your counterpart to climb down or concede the extreme position or ultimatum that they've imposed. If you focus on that ultimatum and start to debate it, then it crystallises and gives it more weight and credence than it deserves. If you can, ignore or downplay it ('I can understand why you might feel like that right now, but let's park that while we focus on some of the things in this deal we *can* agree to'). This means that, when the time comes, your counterpart can take a more moderate position without feeling like they are having to make a big embarrassing U-turn.

Ultimatums are often just used to bully or apply pressure and, frequently, the stated threats never materialise.

4. Moving the goalposts

This can be extremely annoying. But be calm and, again, identify and label what has happened. State clearly that they have changed an agreed point.

A common response from a negotiator who has moved the goalposts can be to hide behind the idea that 'nothing is agreed until everything is agreed'. But this can be countered by saying that's not necessarily true, as you need fixed points to make progress. Request an acknowledgement of their change of position and make it clear that you either can't agree or want a concession in return. The balance of the deal has changed.

If *you* need to move the goalposts: apologise, acknowledge and clarify why you have no choice and what, exactly, your new position is. Expect negotiations to take a little longer.

5. Is there anybody out there?

The problem of non-repliers is a really common issue, especially where you're dealing with a busy negotiator, or where your deal isn't at the top of their to-do list. But it's essential to find out quickly if the silence is because they're just too busy or if it's because the deal isn't going to happen, that way you can make other plans if needs be.

If you need to get a response: email saying you will phone, then phone, leaving a message if there's no answer. Then email again. Then call again. Persistent, polite, patient, but never angry. Angry can put the other party off and give your counterpart an excuse for non-cooperation.

If you're still not having success you could copy in the other side's colleagues or their boss ... but that should be a last resort. How would you feel if someone did this to you?

Another good strategy if you're being ignored is to email with a simple question that is easy for them to answer, for example, 'What further information do you need in order to get back to me?' or 'When realistically do you expect to be able to get back to me?' or even, 'Are you abandoning this deal?' They might be more inclined to send a quick response that will restart the dialogue.

We don't use these types of emails every day, but when the occasion calls for it (for example, when the other side has gone silent for months, without any kind of response despite repeated chasing), it's extraordinary how effective it is — even if it's something that invites a simple answer of 'No ...' (the deal is still on). The psychology is to do with not wanting to admit to having quit something. By eliciting a response, you have re-established communication and are on the way to getting the deal moving again.

6. Boredom

Still no reply or just slow and unhelpful? Consider your alternatives (BATNA). Never contribute to any delay; respond promptly. Again, you can ask the question: 'Do you wish to continue?' Or see if you can find that out by other means. Is there a colleague of theirs who you can speak to informally about what's going on?

Consider and possibly start to take more concrete steps to explore your other options. You may choose to make this obvious to the other side, which might provoke a response. Either way, it will avoid a desperate search down the line if this deal does fail to materialise.

7. Let me check with my boss

This is where your counterpart claims to have no instructions or no authority to progress the deal. Look out for signs of no authority right from the start. If it is going to be a problem, you may as well know as soon as possible.

One approach is to repeat conversations/proposals/ summaries and then ask your counterpart to get points 'signed off' by their boss/colleagues/client (the shorthand we shall use for this person is just the 'principal'). For example, 'Can I take it that this point is agreed so we can progress on this basis?' This may help to flush out what authority/instructions (or a lack of) your counterpart has.

8. Backseat negotiators

Either you or your counterpart may have a principal with very strong ideas about the deal, who is giving instructions from the wings. It's almost always the case that those people are less bullish when they're actually 'in the room' for the negotiation.

If it's *your* principal who is doing the backseat driving, manage their expectations, talk openly to them about your ZOPA and your BATNA in preparation, and get their buy-in to the likely range of outcomes. Keep them copied in (bcc'd if they'd prefer) on any emails to ensure your principal remains engaged and aware of the way in which things are progressing, and to ensure they cannot claim they did not know what was going on.

Even if you don't necessarily agree with your principal's position, try to ensure you represent the determination of what they're asking for. Avoid phrases such as 'my instructions are' as it can easily be taken as shorthand for,

'I don't agree with what my principal is asking for'.
This clearly undermines your negotiating position.

If you suspect your counterpart has a strong-willed principal hiding in the wings, try to draw them out of the shadows and bring them directly into the negotiation: 'Can the principal join us on our call so I can understand their position on this?' Sometimes the invite alone can gain a concession.

9. Mistake paralysis

If you make a mistake in a negotiation, tell someone immediately. Ideally, if you're working in a team, you would discuss this with one of your colleagues initially, but if it's just you, seek the thoughts of someone outside of the negotiation who you trust to provide an objective viewpoint. If the deal is unconcluded, once you have discussed it internally or with a trusted person, tell the other side straight away. The longer you leave it the more difficult it gets. Apologise clearly. No embarrassment needed, we all do it sometimes — don't believe anyone who tells you otherwise!

If your counterpart makes a glaring mistake and you spot it, don't be shy about pointing it out. Do so politely and with the right intentions. If you cut them some slack, make it clear you would expect the same and ensure that it is logged as an indication of trust and collaboration.

You can minimise the chances of mistakes in a complex negotiation by summarising agreed terms (preferably on an ongoing basis). Before it is signed, bring in someone with a fresh pair of eyes to compare a summary with the draft agreement. Decide the most crucial elements and prioritise checks on those.

This book doesn't allow for an exhaustive list of every difficulty that you might encounter in your negotiations. But hopefully these three simple steps will help you to address difficulties in your negotiations:

1. **Acknowledge and accept that, within any negotiation, there will be obstacles to overcome**

2. **Learn to clearly and consistently identify and label those difficulties**

3. **Develop strategies for overcoming such difficulties, one at a time**

If you identify a difficulty and you don't know how to approach it, ask a colleague or someone you trust for their thoughts and ideas. In our years of doing this job, we've yet to find a problem that couldn't be overcome in one way or another. As the title of Ryan Holiday's modern take on stoicism proclaims, *The Obstacle is the Way*.

As you develop your own playbook for navigating these bumps in the road, don't be afraid to keep notes. They may save you time and headaches when you encounter the same difficulties in the future.

10
Find hidden value

In Chapter 8, we looked at the importance of collaboration. Collaboration is a precursor to the fundamental notion of maximising the amount of value that both parties can unlock from any given negotiation.

Let's look back at the model that we deployed in Chapter 1, the idea of the tangled ball of string, and expand on that metaphor. If you're looking to get red string from the ball, just jumping in and grabbing what you see right in front of you is going to yield sub-par results. Because you're only looking at the string on the surface of the ball, not considering what might lie beneath that.

You're also not considering what your counterpart in this exercise wants.

You know they like blue string and that might yield opportunities to exchange any red string that they claim for some blue string that happens to sit on your side of the ball.

But what about the secondary items? You know you could use some orange string. Maybe your counterpart is willing to part with some of that too.

However, would you trade your small stash of blue string (that you know to be valuable to your counterpart) for something like this orange, that is less valuable than your favourite red string? You have an inkling that your counterpart, over there on the other side of the big ball, is picking out other colours, not just blue. Is that some green you can see? Or purple? It's hard to make out from over here.

This kind of asymmetric information is the default state at the beginning of most negotiations. You're likely to have an imperfect notion of what your counterpart's needs and wants are, and how they rank and value those things.

What's less obvious, is that you probably don't have a clear understanding of your own aspirations in the negotiation.

We probably all go into a deal instinctively with a notion of what the most important things are to us in that particular situation. But when a negotiation includes multiple variables, it becomes very difficult to apply any sense of *relative value* between the competing factors in the deal.

Relative values

There is a painting called *The Blue Cart* by Tristram Hillier, a slightly surreal rural scene depicting a farmyard containing a gaily-coloured cart and a church in the distance.

The law firm that Richard used to worked at in Covent Garden had a tatty-looking print of it in one of its meeting rooms. There was an office clear-out one day, and it was added to a pile to be scrapped or claimed by anyone who wanted it.

Richard took it home, drawn to its clash of oddness and familiarity.

A few years later he moved to Somerset and discovered that Tristram Hillier had lived most of his later life in a small village just down the road called East Pennard. The painting took on new significance and meaning. Now, when he's out walking his dog or riding his bike, he keeps an eye out for the barns and church depicted in the scene. He hasn't found them yet, but will keep looking ...

The painting hadn't changed. But its value to Richard had.

What's in a name?

Tina Turner was 39 years old when she finally faced her then husband, Ike Turner, in court. After years of an abusive marriage, she was on the cusp of winning her freedom. But on paper, it wasn't looking like a great deal.

The singer had been left with all the kids, but none of the assets. She had crippling debts and a singing career that looked like it could be on its last legs, especially in an industry that can notoriously favour youth over experience.

When the judge asked Tina what she wanted, she mentioned some jewellery that she had left at the marital home. But when Ike challenged this, she could see which way the negotiation was headed. She famously proclaimed that Ike could keep everything. Apart from her name.

She'd been born Anna Mae Bullock, but the name Tina Turner was the one that she'd become famous with. At the time of the divorce, if you'd been asked to value that name (and artists' names can of course carry a high brand value), any outside observer would have probably placed a relatively low value on it. Certainly less valuable than the catalogue of Ike and Tina's prior recordings, which Ike insisted on retaining.

Indeed, Ike didn't place a high value on letting her keep it. He possibly liked the idea that she would keep the name he'd given her. But from Tina's perspective, the name represented more. It not only represented liberation, but also a platform for *opportunity*. Like buying the rights to a plot of land with the potential to build a magnificent villa. She had the self-belief to know that she could build back a better career than the one she'd walked away from.

In 2021, Tina Turner signed a deal worth reportedly more than $50 million, granting music company BMG the rights to monetise her post-Ike catalogue of music as well as an 'extensive portfolio of rights' related to her name and image. Self-belief and projecting beyond the immediate opportunity had yielded the most valuable outcome for her.

Maximising value

Value is a strange and nebulous concept. As the examples above show, it depends greatly on your own perceptions and attitudes. At the outset of a negotiation, the value that you and your counterpart place on different aspects of a deal may not be at all apparent to each other. Consider a simple record deal that contains just three key variables.

1. The size of the advance
2. The level of the royalty
3. The length of time that the rights will be retained

If we asked the record label and the artist to 'score' the value they place on each of these respective items, the answers are likely to vary.

The artist may score it as follows:
1. The size of the advance — high importance
2. The level of the royalty — mid importance
3. The length rights — low importance

The record label may score it as follows:

1. The size of the advance — low importance
2. The level of the royalty — high importance
3. The length rights — mid importance

Think back to the image of the ZOPA that we explored in chapters 4 and 6. Each of these variables will have their own ZOPA.

Where the negotiation ends up within that ZOPA will ultimately have a very different value based on the relative importance and value that the two parties place on that particular variable.

The advance in this example has a higher relative value to the artist than it does to the label. So, if this variable ends up closer in the deal to the artist's top-end aspirations than it does to the label's best-case scenario, there is a multiplier effect — the actual value here starts to become maximised.

Applying this across the other variables in the deal, it becomes clear that there is a combination of small victories on both sides that will add up to vastly more value being created and captured than if each party doggedly seeks to 'win' each point for the sake of it or by lazily 'splitting the difference'.

This is what we should be striving for consistently in negotiations: having the courage and curiosity to work out what's really important to each party involved in the negotiation, creating as much combined value as you can, and then allocating and claiming it as optimally as possible between the parties.

Stone soup

One of our favourite illustrations of how value can be created, seemingly from thin air, is found in the old folk tale of 'Stone Soup'.

Once upon a time, a group of strangers arrives in a small village, carrying nothing but an empty cooking pot. But the villagers won't share any food with the hungry travellers. So these out-of-towners go to the stream and fill their pot with water. And they throw in a couple of big stones.

One of the villagers asks what they're doing, and they reply, 'We're making stone soup. Never heard of it? You don't know what you're missing! It's delicious, but this batch still needs a bit of seasoning. Be a pal, and go and get us some carrots, would you? You can have a bowl when it's done.'

Off the villager hops, and duly returns with some carrots.

Another villager appears and asks what's going on. And the travellers again tell their story, and that the soup is still lacking that certain something. So, off that villager goes, and returns with some garlic.

And so it goes on. More villagers, more garnish. Potatoes, onions, salt, cabbage, peas, corn, chicken.

Finally, the stones are removed from the pot, and a hearty bowl of soup is enjoyed by all the travellers and the villagers alike.

A win/win plucked from the ether!

11
Enriching relationships

You could say that the world of farming and the music industry couldn't be more different. However, in his 2008 book, *Outliers*, Malcolm Gladwell talks about two different types of culture within farming communities around the world: the 'culture of honour' and the 'culture of cooperation'. And it's the latter that we're interested in here.

Gladwell identifies a culture of honour emerging when, due to the harshness of a landscape, farmers raise goats or sheep instead of farming crops. They must protect that flock at all costs, aggressively warding off threats of it being killed or stolen.

In more fertile areas, a culture of cooperation tends to arise. Here prosperity depends not on warding off threats (unless someone is willing to steal an entire field of crops) but on cooperation and collaboration with your neighbours and the wider community.

Richard's grandfather, Bill Salter, knew a great deal about the culture of cooperation. As a dairy farmer in Devon (and chairman of the local branch of the National Farmers' Union), Richard learned early that:

- Farmers can drive a notoriously hard bargain (as any good tractor salesman will tell you)

- But they do so against the backdrop of needing to maintain long-term, cooperative relationships with those around them

- If you're dishonest or untrustworthy, you will be found out

- Over generations, your good name and reputation come to count for more than a quick buck

- You can be firm and tenacious, without being deceitful or tarnishing your reputation

Isolated interactions or tricky negotiations that might be viewed as difficult or challenging can — when set in the framework of a long-term requirement to collaborate and get along with our neighbours — lead to robust discussions that can see relationships deepen and actually flourish.

Farming communities such as Grandad Bill's vividly illustrate these types of dynamic tensions, and also encapsulate the value of equitable and reciprocal working relationships.

Richard's family has always seemed slightly bewildered at what he does for a living. It's not surprising. The portrayal of the music business in the media often focuses on larger-than-life characters such as the overbearing manager, the diva popstar or the exploitative record label; and the more asymmetrical dynamics of people 'pulling a fast one.'

But there's another side to the industry too. We believe that the modern music business has far more in common with these 'cultures of cooperation' — built on the newfound abundance of opportunity that has accompanied the advent of streaming — than it has with the culture of honour (although that's not to say there aren't still a few sheep rustlers out there!).

Bonobo × Ninja Tune

Simon Green is better known by his stage name, Bonobo. In a career that spans 20 years and six albums, he has gone from underground cult status to worldwide acclaim, both for his recordings — and multiple Grammy award nominations — and his jaw-dropping world tours. Quite a journey for this mild-mannered musician, who at heart remains tirelessly devoted to his craft.

In 2001, Bonobo signed to the UK independent record label Ninja Tune, a label founded by the artist Coldcut in 1990, in part as a reaction to the experiences that they had had under a major record label. They have worked together ever since.

We spoke with Gerard Cantwell (who co-manages Bonobo alongside Randy Reed) and Peter Quicke, currently chair of Ninja Tune, about this longstanding partnership, and their thoughts on a more collaborative approach to negotiation over such a lengthy period of time.

What emerged very quickly in the conversation was that neither Peter nor Gerard consider they are on opposite sides of the bargaining table. Instead — and it would be easy to be cynical about this, but even on a Zoom call the sincerity is very apparent — both the management team and label team have the same perspective: *the interests and success of the artist come first.* There's a mutual respect and a shared understanding that everyone in the relationship needs to play their own role impeccably in order to create a situation in which the artist can thrive.

In the 15 years or so since we've been working together (we are Bonobo's lawyers), we've had various negotiations with Ninja Tune. But tellingly, rather than becoming more strained and complex as time has gone on, the relationship has matured into one of trust and collaboration. In fact, at the time of writing this book, we've just finished a renegotiation relating to his sixth album, *Fragments*, and it has been a very simple and straightforward process.

There are probably a dozen or so well-funded and established labels who might have leapt at the chance to work with Simon on this record. But rather than take a short-term perspective, the artist, management team and label have leaned in to their existing relationship, and built on it. As well as the Bonobo album, they are also collaborating on developing the careers of a number of other artists under Bonobo's Outlier Recordings label imprint.

In many negotiations, it's tempting to consider things in terms of 'them and us'. But, as we've seen throughout this book, it is helpful to reframe this in terms of serving a higher shared cause:

— In this example, it's the label and the management serving the artist

— In the Eavises versus the Mutoids, the bigger picture was the long-term flourishing of the Glastonbury Festival

— In Professor Washington Okumu's example from earlier in the book, the higher cause was the future of South Africa

With this shared mindset, and after one or more fruitful negotiations with a person or a business, what we end up creating — along with all that hidden value we have untangled along the way — is something that it is hard to put a price on, as it plays such a huge and important role in these dealings ... a *shared history*.

It's this shared history that enriches our relationships immeasurably. For better or worse, when we have achieved something together, whether that is in the negotiation itself, or in the work that comes after that, we form stronger bonds, and can achieve what might have once felt impossible.

As we wrap up the conversation with Gerard and Peter, we touch on Malcolm Gladwell's 'two types of culture' model. Peter, it turns out, is also from a long line of Devon dairy farmers. So, while our shared history would seem to go back around 15 years to when we started working with Bonobo, it perhaps goes even deeper. Our grandfathers will almost certainly have negotiated with one another on market day many decades ago.

So, there is a subtle distinction to be drawn here. Long-term relationships don't mean the same thing as long-term deals. Richard remembers being at school and hearing on the news about Jamiroquai (his favourite artist at the time) signing a record deal for something like ten albums. It sounded incredible. Only later would he find out that signing a deal like that at an early stage in an artist's career isn't such a great thing!

In many instances, a successful long-term relationship is often built of much shorter-term contractual tie-ins. This means that the standing of the parties can flex and flow as the relationship develops. The relationship we have with our clients, for instance, only lasts for as long as we're both happy to keep working together. That means that the service and value we provide has to constantly evolve to keep step with the expectations of our clients.

12
Done deal

We were taught early on that once a deal has been done, it's often a good idea to take your counterpart out for lunch for a debrief. This always seemed like a fun thing to do at the end of a successful negotiation, the popping of champagne corks and all that jazz, but it seemed much less appealing at the end of a difficult negotiation.

If a negotiation has been protracted or particularly challenging, it's worth reflecting on it or even doing some analysis. This will help your future negotiations. Start by asking yourself, what could I have done differently or better to get the deal done? In terms of the longer-term working relationship, can you say with certainty that there are no hard feelings now that you've reached an agreement? If an issue comes up with the deal in, say, a year's time, would you want that to be the first time you've spoken to your counterpart since wrangling with them during the negotiations?

For all of these reasons, a cordial face-to-face meeting after a tricky negotiation is often a very good idea.

We've looked at a variety of different negotiations in this book. And in those examples the quality and the duration of the relationship between the parties varies enormously.

At one end of the scale, we had our theoretical interaction with a trader on a far-flung tourist beach haggling over the price of a souvenir. An example where two people were likely never to see each other again. So, in terms of the negotiation, most of the concepts that we've looked at are off the table. There is no ongoing relationship or reputation to consider.

Further along this scale we met the *Love Island* contestants from our chapter on collaboration. They have a relationship, of sorts, but for how long we're not sure yet. Already, though, they find themselves unknowingly drawn to displaying characteristics of collaboration and cooperation.

Further along still, we find the example of Ninja Tune and Bonobo, and the relationship that they have fostered over a span of 20 years and six albums. We notice patterns starting to emerge, based on values of equality, empathy and mutual respect.

Taking this further, we consider the Eavis family, and how their long-term outlook has helped to foster the types of resilient, organic relationships that have enabled them to cultivate one of the best music and arts festivals in the world, over a 50-year time frame.

Or the example of Professor Washington Okumu, who succeeded in a life-or-death negotiation by asking its participants to consider the consequences in the widest possible historical context.

In the conclusion to this book, we want to explore the outer reaches of this idea: that the more long-term and interdependent we view our working relationships, the better our negotiations are apt to become.

So, we spoke to Bella.

Bella is one of six partners in a unique business. It's a business that has been in the same continuous family ownership for 350 years.

That is remarkable in itself. But more unusually, the business is constituted as an 'unlimited liability company'. Most businesses registered at Companies House carry the designation 'limited'. That means that the liability of the companies' owners can't exceed the investment that the owners have put into the company. Put simply, if the business goes bust, the owners won't lose their homes.

This isn't the case for Bella and her six cousins who preside over the 11th generation of the family business. The success or failure of the business, and the fortunes of their customers, are inextricably linked to their own fate.

They are proud to have a relatively small but select list of customers. Notable former clientele include Samuel Pepys, Lord Byron and Jane Austen. Bella is far too discreet to give me any information on current customers. But, speaking to her, it becomes apparent that negotiations with their potentially very demanding customers are actually surprisingly cordial and straightforward. When we speak about the reasons for this, some familiar trends start to appear:

1. They are extremely careful about who they work with. Not everyone can become a customer, and all potential new customers will meet with at least one of the partners to establish if there is a good 'fit'.

2. This means that in the rare situations where there is friction between the business and its customers, the instinctive first response will always be to lean into the relationship, rather than to enforce contractual obligations or similar — such action would always be a matter of last resort.

3. There's a degree of equality in the relationship. Their customers are often extremely successful or wealthy people, but Bella's business is no slouch itself—overseeing billions of pounds of deposits, with annual profits in the eight-figure bracket.

4. This leads naturally to a high degree of empathy and understanding between the parties.

5. These relationships are built from the outset with a long-term outlook; they consider relationships not in terms of years, but in terms of generations.

The negotiations with their customers may be straightforward on the whole but, as anyone who has watched the HBO series *Succession* will tell you, often the trickiest negotiations can come from within your own ranks.

We discussed with Bella how, in the 1890s, the then senior partner in the firm nearly destroyed it.

Charlie Arthur, seventh-generation partner, had little interest in the day-to-day running of the business.

He preferred instead to gamble on horses or, when that was frowned upon, on the stock market, with disastrous losses. After a series of near-ruinous high-profile scandals, he was finally persuaded to step down from his role. But his standing in the organisation allowed him to do so on extremely generous terms that continued to hurt the profits of the family business for years to come.

Rather than treat this reckless figure with scorn or distaste, Bella is more sanguine. She actually sees those exploits as having safeguarded the future of the organisation. Because, having encountered those difficulties, and risks, the organisation followed steps that were remarkably similar to those we encountered in chapter 9 on overcoming difficulties: they recognised them for what they were, and then codified strategies for dealing with the same difficulties again into the company's constitution, so the mistakes of the past couldn't be repeated in the future.

This means that for the current generation of partners the risk is removed; if a partner behaved in the way Charlie Arthur did, they would be out on their ear, and certainly wouldn't get to write their own ticket.

We find all of this particularly fascinating, not only because Bella and her family's business exemplify so many of the ideas that we've explored in this book, but also because the rogue, Charlie Arthur, who nearly sank the business in the 1890s, was Richard's paternal great-great-grandfather.

Bella Hoare and her cousins run C. Hoare & Co., reputedly the fifth oldest private bank in the world. Charlie Arthur's behaviour ensured that Richard's branch of the family tree was quite rightly pollarded, and so his background and upbringing and Bella's were worlds apart.

Not that you would have guessed it from our video call. Rather than focusing on the sins of the fathers, we were more interested in common ground. Bella's stepdaughter Laura has been doing work experience with us, as she's keen to become an entertainment lawyer. Another of the partners at the Bank, Simon, is a keen record collector and used to run a jazz-funk reissue label out of Paris in the 1990s. Richard and Simon swap notes on rare vinyl.

Although Bella, and the bank, are an unusual example, having been in business for 350 years, we believe that we can all do more to consider the long-term implications of our negotiations and relationships. There isn't an *expectation* that all relationships should mirror those of a centuries-old bank and its venerable customers. But that doesn't mean it shouldn't be an *aspiration*.

As we said at the start of this book, there isn't a mythical end point at which negotiation is somehow mastered. It's a lifelong journey, and we hope that some of the ideas in these pages will have provided food for thought.

We hope you can approach your negotiations with energy, enthusiasm, curiosity, gratitude and courage. They are an opportunity not only to try to uncover and distribute the maximum amount of value available to you and your counterparts, but also to build long-lasting and fruitful relationships along the way. Good luck!

'But who has won?'

This question the Dodo could not answer without a great deal of thought, and it sat for a long time with one finger pressed upon its forehead ... while the rest waited in silence.

At last the Dodo said, '*Everybody* has won, and all must have prizes.'

Lewis Carroll, *Alice's Adventures in Wonderland*

Resources

Books

Atomic Habits: An easy and proven way to build good habits and break bad ones
James Clear

Bargaining for Advantage: Negotiation strategies for reasonable people
G. Richard Shell

Versions of his test are available online, try searching 'Negotiating Style Assessment Tool' or 'Bargaining Style Assessment Tool'

Getting to Yes: Negotiating an agreement without giving in
Roger Fisher & William Ury

Meditations
Marcus Aurelius

Negotiating the Impossible: How to break deadlocks and resolve ugly conflicts (without money or muscle)
Deepak Malhotra

Professor Malhotra is well worth following for cutting-edge and topical insights on negotiation: *twitter.com/Prof_Malhotra*

Never Split the Difference: Negotiating as if your life depended on it
Chris Voss

Nonzero: History, evolution & human cooperation
Robert Wright

The Obstacle is the Way: The ancient art of turning adversity to advantage
Ryan Holiday

Operating Manual for Spaceship Earth
R. Buckminster Fuller

Outliers: The story of success
Malcolm Gladwell

The Spotify Play: How CEO and founder Daniel Ek beat Apple, Google, and Amazon in the race for audio dominance
Sven Carlsson and Jonas Leijonhufvud

Start with No: The negotiating tools that the pros don't want you to know
Jim Camp

Stone Soup
Marcia Brown

Thinking, Fast and Slow
Daniel Kahneman

The Tipping Point: How little things can make a big difference
Malcolm Gladwell

Win Win: How to get a winning result from persuasive negotiations
Derek Arden

The Yes Book: The art of better negotiation
Clive Rich

Negotiations in Film & TV

Glastonbury
Julian Temple, 2006
Michael Eavis / The Mutoids scene

Succession
HBO series

True Grit
The Coen Brothers, 2010
Mattie Ross scene

What's Love Got to Do with It
Brian Gibson, 1993

Podcasts

Negotiations Ninja
Mark Raffan

The Sun King
David Dimbleby on Rupert Murdoch

Setlist
Complete Music Update (CMU)

The Golden Rule episode
Radiolab
wnycstudios.org/podcasts/radiolab/ segments/golden-rule
Analysis of one of the strangest 'split or steal' moments in *Golden Balls'* history

About the authors

Both Richard and Andrew are lawyers working within the music industry.

Richard runs Hoare Associates, which he established five years ago after a decade working at Clintons. Based in Somerset, they maintain an extremely high quality and diverse roster that currently includes AJ Tracey, Burial, Bonobo, Kelis, and Glastonbury Festival. He is a graduate of Harvard Business School's 'Negotiation Mastery' programme.

Since qualifying as a barrister in 2005, **Andrew** has worked with key companies in the music industry including records and music publishing (EMI, Virgin Records, Warner/Chappell, Mushroom Records, Boosey & Hawks and Imagem) across all genres of music. He is currently part of Pink Floyd's management team, director of the classical record label Coro, and advisor to individual artists — he is also the person Richard turns to when he hits a particularly tricky negotiation.

Between them, they have more than 50 years' worth of negotiation and music business experience and a reputation for getting the right deal done, without a fuss, and without leaving both parties feeling bruised and battered. They also run a six-week online 'Music Business Negotiation' course.

Thanks

Richard: Thanks to all of the family, friends, clients, colleagues and counterparts who have played their part in the ideas and practices that we have included in this book. Particular thanks go to the remarkable small team I have been privileged to work with through the ups and downs of the past few years: Giselle, Jen, Mitch, Ridley and Sophie. Huge thanks to Miranda West for her patience, wisdom and humour, and for giving us this opportunity. And to James Victore who absolutely nailed the essence of our approach to deal-making on the cover with his emphatic exclamation mark! Above all, my thanks go to the 'wellspring of my confidence' (I pinched that from an episode of *Mad Men*): Rowena, Reggie and Jago.

Andrew: Thank you to all the great people I have had the pleasure of working with in the industry and to my wife, Ann, for putting up with it all.

Books in the series

Also available

Available in print, digital and audio formats from booksellers or via our website: **thedobook.co**

To hear about events and forthcoming titles, you can find us on social media **@dobookco**, or subscribe to our newsletter